How To

FINANCE A HOME

In Oregon

H. L. KIBBEY

Panoply Press, Incorporated
Lake Oswego, Oregon

Cover design and illustrations: Byron Kibbey

Editor: Cynthia Fischborn

ISBN #   0-9615067-0-9

Printed in the United States of America

Panoply Press, Inc.
P. O. Box 1885
Lake Oswego, Oregon 97034

ACKNOWLEDGMENTS

My name appears on the cover of this book, but the project never could have been completed without the help of so many others. First, a thank you to Byron Kibbey, whose design skills produced a striking cover and beautifully readable charts. Throughout the past several months, Cynthia Fischborn's patient and enthusiastic editing has been very much appreciated. Then there are those whose support, encouragement and professional advice merit a hearty round of applause: to Marlys and Dean Burn, Bill Galvin, Darlene Hess, Margie Jones, Cheryl Long, Kaja Voldbaek, Kelly Hepner and Carol Jackson, my sincere thanks. Finally, I would like to express my appreciation to my clients who, over the years, have given me a wealth of experience and a reason to write.

Buying, selling or refinancing a home is an important transaction that should be researched thoroughly. Learn to rely on a team of professional advisors: your real estate agent, loan officer, accountant and attorney to give you the help you will need. I am a real estate agent and can write only from that viewpoint. The information in this book, while carefully compiled, is not intended to be used as a substitute for competent professional or legal advice. Remember that financing facts and figures are subject to change.

To Tristania, Tohren and Byron.

TABLE OF CONTENTS

Part I

How, Where And Why

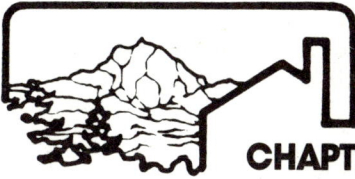

CHAPTER 1

Why This Book?

Buying a home is the great American dream. It's a tradition that is just as sacred as motherhood and apple pie. On the other hand, financing that home today has become a nightmare, a thoroughly mystifying ritual with special rules and jargon all its own.

Novice, first-time buyers are not alone in their bewilderment. With the number of different types of home mortgage loans increasing at an astounding rate, even seasoned borrowers have difficulty absorbing all the changes. A typical lender might offer dozens of home loans with almost infinite variations on the theme.

Multiply this by twenty or thirty lenders and you can see how the dilemma is compounded. Now add in the many types of government loans that are available and the different ways to use "creative" financing. The total number of possibilities could overwhelm even the staunchest home buyer.

We would all like to be educated consumers. No one wants to spend $5000 in loan fees to finance a home, only to discover later that there was a much better way of doing it. Until now, it has been very difficult, in fact almost impossible, to 'comparison shop' the many possible ways of financing a home. You can visit a handful of lending institutions, read every article in the real estate section of the newspaper, contact government agencies and, weeks later, still not have found the best loan for you.

That is why I wrote this book. If it helps you avoid a costly financing mistake, if it suggests a new way for you to buy or sell a home, if it removes home loans from the list of Mysteries of Life, then I've accomplished my goal.

"My friend got a great assumption . . . "
At any social gathering I've ever attended, the conversation has shifted, sooner or later, to real estate. I once thought, rather immodestly, that because I was a real estate agent, my mere presence in the room would guarantee a delicious debate about interest rates and contract terms. Surely every ear anxiously awaited my words of wisdom.

Somehow I learned that my presence had very little to do with the flow of conversation. Homebuying (or selling) is a topic so close to everyone's heart and pocketbook that real estate jargon has become a second language. It's not surprising to hear the same collection of thoughts brought out at each party, to be mulled over and reaffirmed by well-meaning friends.

"Contracts are the way to go."
"Don't even mention graduated-payment loans."
"I want an 8 percent assumption."
"Oh, we'd never go to a mortgage company; our banker knows us."

Those may be perfectly valid statements; they are also potentially disastrous. The best way to finance your friend's home is probably not the best method for you. Forget the time-honored expression, "What's sauce for the goose is sauce for the gander"; in real estate, it just isn't so.

This should be Rule #1 on any list of financing do's and don'ts: research the market to find a home loan that fits your needs, not one that 'everyone' is talking about. Be open to new ideas in financing. You may end up with the type of loan you've always had, or you may discover a different kind of loan that makes more economic sense to you.

There are other rules that are also important and they are listed at the end of this chapter. To give you a colorful example of what can happen when you ignore them, here is the case history of *Chuck and Marianne Brent. Within the space of four years, the Brents broke

All names used in the case histories have been changed to avoid embarrassment.

every rule on the list! They financed and refinanced their home three times, at a cost of over $8,000, and are still far from happy with their final loan.

Case History: The Brents

When Chuck and Marianne Brent found their dream home, interest rates on mortgages were hovering around 14%. It was a new home, still under construction, on the edge of a wooded ravine. The Brents were concerned about the interest rates, but the builder reassured them, "Don't worry, I'll sell it to you on contract". At that time, the fashionable word was 'contract'. Contracts were touted as the magic elixir to cure all financing pains. The Brents were delighted.

There was, however, a catch: because the builder had a temporary construction loan, the best he could offer (with his lender's permission) was a contract for only one year, at an interest rate of 13%. At the end of the year, the Brents would have to obtain a new loan. It was a gamble that the Brents decided to take. After all, interest rates couldn't stay high for ever.

So Chuck and Marianne bought on contract, moved in and waited for the interest rates to drop. Instead they soared to the lofty heights of 16% to 17% by the time the year was over. The Brents were appalled. They could have taken time then to research the loan market thoroughly but instead they grasped at what, to them, seemed like a life raft. The bank that held the underlying construction loan offered stop-gap financing: a three-year loan at 15% interest. Relieved, the Brents paid the loan fees and closing costs, and settled back again, hoping for a miracle in three years.

The interest rates did drop, and Chuck and Marianne quickly applied for permanent financing. Once again, they did not shop for the best possible loan. They went back to the same bank and refinanced the home with a 30-year fixed-rate mortgage at 13¾%, again paying all necessary fees. As Marianne said, "The loan officer knew us by then and knew our payment history. We saved the appraisal fee of $125 and it was so much easier not to shop around. We were sure we were getting a good rate."

Happy ending? Not quite. Here's why:
The dream home, for which the Brents originally paid $81,500, by then had cost them almost $90,000 if we include the non-recoverable financing costs. Yet the market value of their home had not risen correspondingly. It was still worth only $81,500.

While 13¾% sounded like music to the Brents' ears, several other lenders had much lower interest rates at the time, and more favorable terms. The appraisal fee of $125 was insignificant compared to what Chuck and Marianne could have saved in loan fees and monthly payments by researching all possibilities.

Their new loan is not assumable and the bank will not permit them to sell their home on contract. Chuck works for a company that transfers its employees every few years. When Chuck is transferred, his firm will not buy his home from him. It will be up to the Brents to find a buyer who is willing and able to get a new loan. If the Brents had kept this in mind, they might have chosen a loan that could be easily assumed by the next buyer (an important factor at times when new loans are difficult to obtain).

It is easy for us to look back at the Brents' decisions and criticize each move. Since we cannot accurately predict the rise and fall of interest rates, mistakes in judgment are still possible. The Brents, however, broke the five basic rules:

RULES TO CONSIDER WHEN FINANCING YOUR HOME

1. Choose the type of financing that is best suited to your income and financial requirements. Don't be swayed by financing fads. A loan that is right for the Joneses may be disastrous for you.

2. Research government loan programs. They offer favorable interest rates and are sometimes easier to qualify for than conventional loans.

3. Once you have decided what type of loan you want, comparison shop for the best possible interest rates, loan fees, terms and conditions. Don't choose a lender just because he knows you.

4. Avoid the need to refinance later. Each time you take out a new loan, you will "lose" a considerable amount of money in the form of loan fees and closing costs. It may be less expensive to choose a long-term loan at a slightly higher interest rate than to refinance your home.

5. Plan for the future. If possible, choose a loan with terms that will be acceptable to you five or ten years from now. If assumability or the right to sell your home on contract is important, find a loan that includes these provisions.

CHAPTER 2

How To Use This Book

This is a book for Oregonians. It was designed to give the homebuyer or seller information about all the financing options available here in Oregon. Of course, some of the information is valid in any state. For example, there are conventional fixed-rate loans and FHA loans everywhere in the country. And people from coast to coast are buying or selling by means of land sales contracts. Certain basic lending principles remain the same wherever you go.

But the similarities end at the basics. Each state has its own unique set of real estate laws and practices; Oregon is no exception. Financing a home in Oregon is a very different matter from financing a home in Georgia, Ohio, Washington or any other state. Not only do interest rates differ and loan limits vary, but even the terminology changes from area to area. For example, 'land sales contracts' in Oregon become 'land contracts' or 'contracts for deed' in other places. Types of loans that are popular in the midwest, for example, may be difficult to find here, or vice versa. Even federal loan programs such as FHA have local variations.

In addition, Oregonians are fortunate to have some wonderful made-in-Oregon loan programs, such as those run by the Department of Veterans' Affairs and the Department of Commerce, Housing Division. Some of the programs and financing techniques in this book will be new to you; others will be familiar. Don't overlook one you have ruled out in the past: things change quickly in the world of finance and a loan program that was wrong for you last year may be perfect today.

A FINANCING OVERVIEW

	Conventional Financing									Government Loans					Other Types Of Financing				
	Fixed-rate 30-year loans	Fixed-rate shorter-term loans	Loans with buydowns	Graduated-payment loans	Loans with calls	Growing-equity mortgage loans (GEMs)	Adjustable-rate mortgage loans (ARMs)	Graduated-payment ARMs	Federal Land Bank Loans	HUD/FHA loans ✱	VA loans ✱	Oregon DVA loans	Single Family Mortgage Purchase Program	FmHA Loans	Seller-financing	Assumptions	Second trust deed loans	Wrap loans	Sweat equity
Fixed interest rate	★	★	★	★	★	★				★	★		★	★	★	★	★	★	
Adjustable or variable rate		★		★		★	★	★		★		★			★	★	★		
Level payments	★	★	★	★						★	★		★	★	★	★	★	★	
Varying payments			★	★	★	★	★	★	★	★	★	★			★	★			
Early payoff		★				★	★								★				
Income restriction													★	★					
Low-income subsidy										★					★				
Easier to qualify for			★	★			★	★		★	★	★	★	★	★				
Down payment less than 5%										★	★			★	★				★
No money down											★			★	★	★			★
Jumbo loans	★	★	★		★	★	★	★							★	★			
Refinancing	★	★				★	★	★	★	★	★						★	★	
Loans for veterans										★	★	★							
Loans for first-time buyers										★			★						
Buying a "fixer-upper"										★					★	★			★
Farms/rural housing									★			★		★	★				
Mobile homes		★	★			★	★	★		★	★	★	★		★	★	★		

Pay particular attention to the loans marked ★ . These specifically meet that requirement, although other types of financing may also be suitable.

✱ HUD/FA and VA have a variety of loan programs to meet almost every need. Refer to those chapters for details.

This book gives you the information you will need to study the many financing possibilities and to compare them at a glance. How you use the book depends upon whether you are buying, refinancing or selling a home. However the chart in this chapter is a good place for everyone to start. It will help focus your attention on the types of loans that best fit your needs. It will also eliminate those loan programs that could not possibly work for you. As an example, if you earn $45,000 a year, you can immediately rule out both the FmHA and the Oregon Housing Division programs, since they have income ceilings that are considerably lower.

As you look at the chart, you'll see various methods of financing (and refinancing) across the top. Down the left side is a list of needs, qualifications or requirements a borrower may have. (Sellers, consider the needs of a typical buyer for your home. For example, if yours is a $200,000 home in perfect condition, neither "low income loans" nor "sweat equity" would apply.)

Study each item on the list to see if it matches your situation. If it does, trace a path to the right to discover which loan programs would best solve that need, those marked (*). The chart gives you a broad overview of the loans and other financing techniques that follow. But do not limit your reading to those "most-likely-to-succeed" chapters. Just as each type of financing has evolved from an earlier kind of loan, so the chapters of this book unfold. You will find bits of pertinent information tucked into each one. A prospective borrower who has no interest in government financing may discover a previously unheard-of loan, one that could wrap up a new home with easy terms.

Part II

Conventional Financing

DEFINITION: **A conventional loan is one that is neither insured, guaranteed nor funded by the government.**

I'll admit that's a negative definition, but it is far easier to describe what conventional loans are **not** than to say exactly what they **are**. There are many different sources for conventional financing. While we usually hear this term in reference to institutional loans, that is, non-government loans offered by banks, savings and loans, mortgage companies, mortgage loan brokers and insurance companies, it also applies to loans from private sources.

If you borrow money from a bank to finance a new home, that's a conventional loan. So is the money you borrow from your parents or from your credit union. When offering you the loan, the lender simply studies your assets and liabilities, decides whether or not to give you the money, and accepts security in the form of a mortgage or trust deed on the property.

This transaction is strictly between the borrower and the lender; in conventional financing, the government does not provide the funds or call the shots.

"The Good Old Days"
If I had written this book at any time prior to the late 1970's, my job would have been infinitely easier. Ah! for the good old days when selecting financing was a simple procedure. At that time, the home-buyer had very few decisions to make. The home loans offered by the different institutions varied only slightly from lender to lender. Most were fixed-rate, long-term loans, with equal monthly payments over the life of the loan and wonderfully low interest rates that are just fond memories today. No one needed a book like this.

All of a sudden, the loan picture changed. Rapidly increasing inflation of the 1970's brought growing dissatisfaction to the financial community. Interest rates on home mortgages, which had fluctuated very little over the previous 30 to 40 years, suddenly increased drastically. For instance, the interest rate on FHA loans first reached the double digits (10%) in April 1979. By September 1981, less than 2½ years later, it soared to 17.5%.

No wonder the mortgage lenders were dissatisfied! Those who had provided money at 6% interest on fixed-rate, 30-year loans were locked into that meager 6% return on their investment for the full 30-year term (or until the loan was repaid). But what home buyer wanted to, or could afford to obtain new financing at 17.5% in order to pay off these old loans?

The result was a stalemate, with the lenders wanting to make new loans but needing to charge such high interest rates that the number of borrowers dwindled. Both sides suffered; the lenders were stuck with their old unprofitable loans, while a very large percentage of Americans could not afford to buy a home.

Being amazingly resourceful, the lenders developed compromise plans. They experimented with new varieties of mortgage loans that would satisfy their investment needs, yet would be palatable and affordable enough to encourage borrowing. This has resulted in a bumper crop of new financing ideas such as the shorter term mortgages, the Graduated-Rate Mortgages, Adjustable-Rate Mortgages, Growing Equity Mortgages, buy-downs, balloons, plus an overwhelming number of variations and combinations of these.

The general public is understandably confused. Many home buyers shy away from these innovations simply because they are different and a little more complex than the standard fixed-rate loans. Yet one of these new loans might be the only way for you to buy the home you have your heart set on. Don't rule out any possibility, however unappealing it may seem at first glance. Once you understand the central idea behind each of the different financing options, you will be able to choose the ones which suit your particular needs. The loan programs we will investigate in this book are in their simplest form. Remember that each lender offers variations on the theme, so expect some differences as you talk to different loan officers.

LOAN-TO-VALUE RATIO

Before we study the individual types of loans, let's look at the term 'Loan-to-Value Ratio', otherwise known as LTV or LVR. Since conventional lenders determine the amount of money they will loan you and the interest rate they will charge by your Loan-to-Value Ratio, it is an important term to understand.

Very simply, your LTV is the amount of the loan, compared to the value of the property. It is expressed as a percentage. For example, if we take a $100,000 home and a buyer with a $20,000 down payment:

First we calculate the loan amount needed:

Value of home	$100,000
Less down payment	-20,000
Amount of loan	$ 80,000

Then we can determine the Loan-to-Value Ratio:

$$LTV = \frac{\text{Amount of loan}}{\text{Value of property}} \times 100\%$$

$$= \frac{80,000}{100,000} \times 100\%$$

$$= \quad 80\%$$

If that same buyer had only $10,000 for a down payment, instead of $20,000, his LTV would be 90%. The larger the down payment amount, the lower the LTV.

Lenders prefer larger down payments, and hence, lower LTVs, because statistics show that a buyer who has more of his or her own money invested in the property will be less likely to default on the loan. That means less risk to the lender. So the buyer with a low LTV can usually receive some concessions in return, such as a slightly lower interest rate and no mortgage insurance. This, of course, varies from loan to loan and from lender to lender.

The practice of offering such concessions could turn into an unmanageable situation without a set of guidelines. If borrower A (on the same $100,000 loan) has a down payment of $19,000, while borrower B has only $16,400, just how much of a concession should the lender make? And what about borrower C with $13,000? How much higher should his interest rate be?

Standardizing LTVs

To simplify things, the lending institutions have adopted a standard policy of grouping loans according to their LTVs They have chosen 95%, 90% and 80% as their usual categories and have eliminated all others. Any LTV that falls between two of the categories is placed in the next highest one. Let's look at how this would affect borrowers A, B and C above, buying that $100,000 home:

	Down Payment	Loan Amount	Value of Home	Calculated LTV	LTV Loan Category
A	$19,000	$81,000	$100,000	81%	90%
B	$16,400	$85,600	$100,000	85.6%	90%
C	$13,000	$87,000	$100,000	87%	90%

According to our calculations, all three of these LTVs fall between the 80% and 90% categories. By applying the standard, a lender would consider all three to have a 90% LVR, regardless of the difference in down payment size.

Here's an important point to note. Borrower A is only $1,000 away from an 80% LTV. By increasing his down payment to $20,000, he may be able to save even more than $1,000 at closing or over the life of the loan. That depends upon the differences between his lender's 90% and 80% LTV loans and is something that should be discussed with the loan officer.

What about LTVs higher than 95%?

I cannot name one bank, savings and loan association or mortgage broker that will offer a conventional loan greater than 95% LTV, that is, a loan with a down payment less than 5% of the value. The risk is simply too great. Government-backed loans, even those offered by these same institutions, are a different matter. There the government is willing to shoulder some of that risk, through an insurance or guarantee program, and up to 100% LTV is possible. Any borrower with a down payment of less than 5% should study the section on government financing later in this book.

What determines the value?
Be aware that the value of a piece of property is not necessarily the same figure as the agreed-upon sales price, in the eyes of a lender. After you apply for a loan, the loan officer will order a professional appraisal of the property and will use the results of that appraisal to determine the LTV. If the appraised value agrees with the sales price, all the LTV calculations you and the loan officer have been making will be correct. But if the appraisal comes in low, you will not be able to get as large a loan as you had planned.

We'll take borrowers A, B and C above as an example. The sales price in this case is $100,000 but let's suppose the appraiser estimated the home to be worth only $90,000. That figure, $90,000, is the one the lender will use to calculate the LTV, yet the buyer must still pay the seller $100,000 unless the deal is renegotiated. The chart below shows what a difference this makes in the amount of the loan:

Appraised Value	Maximum 80% LTV Loan	Maximum 90% LTV Loan	Maximum 95% LTV Loan
$100,000	$80,000	$90,000	$95,000
$ 90,000	$72,000	$81,000	$85,500

With the appraised value of $90,000, Borrower A barely squeezes into the 90% LTV category; it would now take an additional $9,000 down payment to obtain an 80% LTV loan. Borrowers B and C, asking for $85,600 and $87,000 loans respectively, now cannot borrow what they need, even with a 95% LTV loan. Both will have to come up with a larger down payment (although in B's case only $100) to obtain a loan.

The Down Payment Approach to LTVs
We have discussed how lenders focus on the amount of the loan as compared to the value of the property. But quite often borrowers like to think in terms of the size of the down payment, rather than the size of the loan. After all, that is the cold, hard cash they have to come

up with. So here is how to determine what your LTV category is, based upon your down payment.

First, calculate your down payment percentage, compared to the value of the home, using the following formula:

$$\text{Down payment \%} = \frac{\text{Down payment \$}}{\text{Value of Home}} \times 100$$

For example, Borrower A above, with a $19,000 down payment and a $100,000 home, has a 19% down payment. Now use the following chart to see what LTV loan category you would be in.

% of Downpayment To Value Of Property	LTV Loan Category
5% to 9.99%	95% LTV
10% to 19.99%	90% LTV
20% and over	80% LTV

PRIVATE MORTGAGE INSURANCE (PMI)

Private mortgage insurance, commonly known as PMI, is as popular among borrowers as the common cold and just as unavoidable for many. It is an insurance policy to protect the investor (lender) against loss suffered if the borrower should default and foreclosure becomes necessary. It does not protect the borrower in any way. PMI is required on most, if not all, conventional loans with an LTV ratio over 80%, and on many of the riskier loans (some graduated-payment loans, for instance), over 75% LTV.

The cost of the insurance is what makes borrowers groan, for they are the ones who foot the bill. The premium is based upon the type of loan (fixed-rate, adjustable-rate, etc.) and the loan-to-value ratio. Loans that carry a higher risk for the investor will have more expensive premiums. In other words, loans with a higher LTV will cost more to insure, as will adjustable-rate loans, especially those with deferred interest (a term that will be explained later).

The first year's PMI premium must be paid at closing and each month thereafter, 1/12th of a year's premium will be paid in the regular monthly loan payment. Here are some sample costs:

Sample 30-year Loans Amount, Type, LTV	Premium Paid At Closing	Monthly Premium
$50,000 fixed-rate 80%	$125	$10
$50,000 fixed-rate 90%	$450	$12
$50,000 fixed-rate 95%	$650	$15
$50,000 adjustable 80%	$325	$16
$50,000 adjustable 90%	$450	$18
$50,000 adjustable 95%	$750	$18

You will note that the first year's premium is usually more expensive than that of the following year. From the second year on, the payment remains the same each month for the life of the loan, or in some policies, the premium is again reduced from the eleventh year on.

Because the premium varies from loan to loan, depending upon the requirements of the loan investor, as well as the risk factor of the loan, it is impossible to give one cost formula that will apply to all situations. When you are ready to finance a home and know the size and type of loan you need, a loan officer can give you an accurate figure.

The only way to avoid mortgage insurance is to make a down payment of more than 20%, or to choose a type of non-conventional financing (a VA or DVA loan, land sales contract etc.) that does not require it.

Now that the preliminary explanations are out of the way, we can move on to discuss the various kinds of conventional financing. The following chapters deal with those types of loans you will encounter in today's market.

CHAPTER 3
Fixed-Rate
30-Year Loans

DEFINITION: **A conventional, fixed-rate 30-year loan has an interest rate that does not vary over the life of the loan.* It has equal monthly payments that include both principal and interest, and is fully amortized. This means that the monthly payments have been calculated so that all principal and interest due will have been completely paid by the end of the 30th year.**

(* Loan documents often list specific circumstances under which the interest rate may increase. These might include sale, lease or transfer of interest in the property, or failure to meet the conditions of the loan agreement. These exceptions vary from loan to loan. Be sure to study all loan documents thoroughly.)

The long-term fixed-rate loan has been "Old Faithful" to generations of borrowers. Since its origin in the 1930s, it has been the most common home-financing method in the United States. Home buyers today use it as a yardstick to measure and evaluate all the other "new-fangled" loan ideas. How does it compare? In some cases, "Old Faithful" does an excellent job of financing a home, but higher interest rates have forced many borrowers to look at other types of loans.

Here's why: let's compare two 30-year loans, one at 6% interest (circa 1972) and one at 13% interest (all too common in the 80s). We'll use as an example a $75,000 home and a borrower with a $10,000 down payment who needs a $65,000 loan. Notice what a difference the interest rate makes in the borrower's monthly payments:

27

	Monthly Payment (Principal & Interest)
6% interest	$390
13% interest	$719

This is quite a hefty difference, but what many prospective borrowers find even more astounding is the amount of income a borrower must earn to qualify for each of these fixed-rate loans. Since the income figure is based on the monthly payment, it's easy to see that an increase in the interest rate will mean an increase in income needed. Following the instructions for qualifying the borrower given in a later chapter, we find that:

Interest Rate	Yearly Income Needed to Qualify For $65,000 Loan*
6%	$23,143
13%	$37,243

* These figures are approximate, for a borrower with little or no other debt. Different homes and debt ratios could require a larger income in both cases.

In other words, in 1972 a borrower needed to earn only $23,143 to obtain a fixed-rate loan. Today that income must be over $14,000 higher, for the same type of loan. No wonder buyers are looking for alternate routes!

Higher interest rates certainly narrow the field of possible borrowers. Since the interest rates lenders charge for their fixed-rate loans are usually higher than that for adjustable-rate loans, a larger income is needed to qualify for a basic fixed-rate loan. That is why "Old Faithful" is not as useful a financing tool as it once was. A borrower whose income is too low to qualify for a fixed-rate loan should consider a buydown, a graduated payment loan, an adjustable rate loan, or any combination of these. They will be explained later in the book.

The Interest Rate Gamble
There are times when a fixed-rate loan is not the answer, even if you can afford it. When interest rates are high, should you lock yourself into a 30-year fixed-rate loan? Or should you gamble on an adjustable-rate, hoping that the interest rates will be lower in the future? One buyer, Tom Linville, played the game and drew a winning hand.

Case History: Tom Linville

Tom was a handsome bachelor in his mid-thirties when he bought one of my listings. This polished gem of a townhouse matched his sophisticated lifestyle perfectly.

When Tom applied for a loan, interest rates were on a hellbent course, straight up. At the time of loan commitment they were 13% for a fixed-rate loan. His friends were of the opinion that the rates had peaked, but his loan officer could only mutter in a pained voice, "I'm not so sure of that."

Tom analyzed the pros and cons of each type of financing available to him. 13% seemed an outrageous rate to pay, although with his income he could certainly afford to do so. Would he regret being tied to a 30-year loan at such a high rate? Perhaps it would be better to choose the lender's adjustable-rate loan at 12% interest. That loan could be converted to a fixed-rate loan within two years and surely rates would be lower by then. But his loan officer advised, "Don't count on it."

Tom finally chose the fixed-rate loan and thereby went down a notch or two in his friends' estimation. But he was kind enough not to rub it in when the rates continued to climb past 14, 16, even 18%! The rates eventually came down, at times dipping a little below Tom's 13% level. The adjustable rate loan would have followed suit in both directions.

Just out of curiosity Tom kept a running comparison of his fixed-rate loan and the adjustable-rate loan he might have chosen. He estimates that he has saved approximately $4000 in the last four years. Yet Tom is realistic enough to admit that his choice was a gamble. . . well reasoned perhaps, but nevertheless a gamble. If 13% had indeed been the peak, the adjustable-rate loan would have been far less expensive.

How Long Will You Own The Home?
Another reason for avoiding a fixed-rate 30-year loan is that you expect to own the home only a short time.

Perhaps you anticipate a company transfer in two years. If so, it may be wiser to opt for an adjustable-rate, saving money with a slightly lower interest rate for the first two years. However, not all adjustable-rate loans will work for this purpose. Be sure to read that chapter thoroughly to avoid the pitfalls and ask your real estate agent or lender to calculate your costs from purchase to resale for different types of loans.

Assumability Of A 30-Year Fixed Rate Loan
If you do expect to sell your home within a few years, the assumability of your loan could be an important factor. Very few of today's 30-year fixed-rate loans are assumable in the way we would like them to be. How convenient it would be for buyers and sellers if the existing loan could be transferred to the new buyer at the existing interest rate.

Today it is very difficult to find a new 30-year fixed-rate loan that is assumable at all. The few that are usually have a clause that gives the lender the right to raise the interest rate to the market rate (or higher) at the time of resale. Lenders do not want to carry old, low interest loans which could be replaced by new, profitable loans.

If the assumability of the loan is important to you, discuss this with the loan officer before signing the loan application. Be sure that you and the loan officer are talking the same language; the word "assumable" can mean different things to different people. Some borrowers simply ask, "Is this loan assumable?" If the answer is "Yes", they are satisfied. Only at closing, when it is time to sign the loan documents, do they realize that certain conditions must be met by the new buyer in order for the loan to be transferred and the interest rate for the new buyer could be double what the original borrowers have paid.

So if your loan officer mentions that your new loan will be "assumable", ask the following questions:

1. Will the interest rate, term and monthly payment remain the same upon assumption?

2. Must the new buyer qualify for the loan? Or may anyone assume the loan, regardless of his or her financial status?
3. What assumption fee will be charged by the lender?
4. What will the seller's liability be after the new buyer has assumed the loan?
5. Are any of these answers subject to change in the future?

The days of "free and easy" assumptions are disappearing quickly, so do not expect to find a liberal assumption policy on a 30-year fixed rate loan. If assumability is of vital importance to you, study the different government loans, such as FHA or VA, and be sure to read the chapter on Assumptions to understand the whole story.

ADVANTAGES OF A FIXED-RATE 30-YEAR LOAN
1. Predictability: Your monthly payments (excluding taxes and insurance) will be exactly the same for the next thirty years. There will be no surprises, no unexpected increases or large balloon payments to plan for.
2. Security: Your loan will not be affected in any way by changes in the economy.

DISADVANTAGES OF A FIXED-RATE 30-YEAR LOAN
1. Higher interest rate: Lenders usually charge a higher interest rate for their fixed-rate loans. (However if rates climb, an adjustable-rate loan could end up at a higher level.)
2. Higher monthly payments: These loans have higher monthly payments (at least initially) than some other types of loans, such as the Graduated Payment and the Adjustable Rate Loans.)
3. More difficult to qualify: Because the monthly payments are higher, a borrower must have a higher income to qualify for a 30-year fixed rate loan, as compared to other types of loans.
4. Long-term commitment: This could be an advantage or disadvantage, depending upon how satisfied you are with your interest rate. If rates decline, you may wish you had chosen an adjustable.

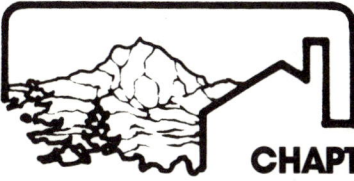

CHAPTER 4

Fixed-Rate
Shorter-Term Loans

DEFINITION: **A conventional fixed-rate shorter-term loan is similar to a fixed rate 30-year loan but has a term that is shorter than 30 years, usually 15 years. It has an interest rate and amortized monthly payments that never vary over the life of the loan.**

If you are fortunate enough to have a higher income than necessary to qualify for a fixed-rate 30-year loan and the ability to make larger monthly payments, this may be just the loan for you!

The Good News . . .
But who wants higher monthly payments? According to loan officers, a surprising number of borrowers choose this method of financing. Here's why: first, they can save 15 years' worth of interest by paying off a loan in 15 years instead of 30. Second, lenders usually offer a lower interest rate on their 15-year loans, thereby increasing the savings.

And The Bad . . .
Of course there are disadvantages too. Because the loan must be repaid in 15 years, the amortized monthly payments are higher. This, in turn, means that a higher income is needed to qualify for the loan.

Quick Build-up Of Equity
Another factor to consider is the speed at which the owner's equity is built up. Since the extra amount paid each month is applied to the principal, the loan balance is reduced much faster than for the 30-year loan. This

sounds like an unquestionable advantage, having a home completely paid for in 15 years. However it could also be a disadvantage if the home is sold.

This is especially significant if the loan is assumable. The greater the owner's equity, the greater the difference between the loan balance and the new sales price. The new buyer assumes the loan but must somehow pay the seller that difference. Most buyers find it easier to assume a larger loan with lower monthly payments and a smaller equity to cash out. In difficult markets, the owner may have trouble getting all of his cash back out of the home.

Comparing 15-year And 30-year Fixed-Rate Loans
Here's a comparison between three $65,000 fixed rate loans, a 30-year loan at 13% interest, and two 15-year loans, one at 13% interest to illustrate the effect of the shorter term, and the other at 12.5% to show the additional interest savings at a lower rate.

	Loan Amount	Interest Rate	Monthly Payment (P&I)	Interest Paid 1st Month	Principal Paid 1st Month	Balance After 1 Month	Total Interest Over Term	Income Needed to Qualify *
30-yr	$65,000	13%	$719	$704	$ 15	$64,985	$193,850	$37,243
15-yr	$65,000	13%	$822	$704	$118	$64,882	$ 83,032	$41,657
15-yr	$65,000	12.5%	$801	$677	$124	$64,876	$ 79,204	$40,757

* Income figures are approximate for a borrower with few or no debts, paying $150 per month property taxes and insurance.

Were you surprised to learn that the monthly payments for the 15-year loan are not twice the size of the 30-year loan payments? In fact, at this interest rate they are only about 14% higher. That reflects the savings in interest over the life of the 15-year.

As you can see, if the interest rate and the loan balance are the same, then the same amount of interest will be due, regardless of the term of the loan. Anything over and above that interest amount will be applied to the principal, thereby lowering the loan balance. You'll notice from the chart that the principal on the 15-year loans has been reduced by over $100 more than that on the 30-year. That's just the first month! Since the loan balance on the 15-year is now lower than the 30-year, the second month will bring a savings in interest, too. (Interest due each month is based on the loan balance; a lower balance will mean a lower amount charged to interest.)

Combining The Best Of Both

If your lender will allow it, you may borrow some of the techniques and advantages of the 15-year loan, to use with your existing 30-year loan. By voluntarily increasing your monthly payment each month, you can reap the interest-saving benefits and at the same time lower your loan balance at a much faster rate. On the other hand, you are not locked into the higher payments and can drop back to the regular amount at any time. This "safety valve" could come in handy if you run into financial difficulties.

A word of warning: be sure to ask your lender's permission to do this. Some loan documents include a penalty for payments beyond the call of duty. That would take the fun and profit out of this technique in a hurry.

Assumability of a Fixed-Rate Shorter-Term Loan

All of the cautions, questions and guidelines discussed in the section on fixed rate 30-year loans apply equally well here. Be sure to read it thoroughly.

Because of the rapid equity build-up, shorter-term loans are not as easy for a new buyer to assume. Not only must the buyer be willing and able to pay the higher monthly payments, but he or she must also have the means to reimburse the owner for his equity. These conditions narrow the field of possible buyers and anyone applying for a shorter-term loan should be aware of this drawback.

ADVANTAGES OF A FIXED-RATE SHORTER-TERM LOAN

1. Dramatic savings in interest (compared to 30-year loan).
2. Usually available at a slightly lower interest rate.
3. Rapid build-up of equity (although this could be a disadvantage at time of sale).

DISADVANTAGES OF A FIXED-RATE SHORTER-TERM LOAN

1. Higher monthly payments.
2. Higher income needed to qualify for the loan.
3. Resale may be more difficult.

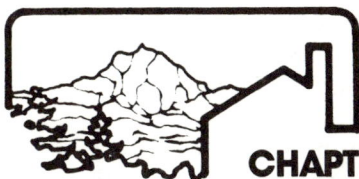

CHAPTER 5
Loans With Buydowns

DEFINITION: **A buydown is a sum of money advanced to the lender at time of closing, in exchange for a reduction in the interest rate of the loan. In effect, a buydown is a form of prepaid interest.**

A buydown is a handy little technique that makes a loan more affordable. With the lowering of the interest rate comes a lower monthly payment and many lenders will use that lower payment as a basis for qualifying the borrower. That means less income is needed to qualify for the loan. Or, to put it another way, a borrower would be able to receive a larger loan than he would have without the buydown.

Sellers, too, should consider the advantages of buydowns. Most lenders will permit anyone to pay the buydown fee: buyer, seller, parents, relatives or fairy godmother. If a seller is willing to foot the bill, the number of potential buyers increases for each percentage point of interest that is bought down. On a $65,000 loan at 13%, for example, reduced to 12%, a borrower would need to earn $2,200 less per year to qualify for the loan. That same 13% loan bought down to 11% would allow a buyer earning $4700 less per year to purchase the home. A buydown will dramatically increase the seller's chances of a sale, especially in a market where buyers are having difficulty getting loans.

Two Kinds Of Buydowns
There are two kinds of buydowns, permanent and temporary. A permanent buydown is one in which the interest rate remains at a constant low level for the entire term of a fixed-rate loan. Permanent buydowns

are also available on some adjustable-rate loans; here the buydown affects the margin for the entire term of the loan. I'll explain more about this later.

A temporary buydown, in comparison, changes the interest rate for only a short time, usually one to three years. After that, the rate returns to its original pre-buydown level, or in the case of an adjustable rate loan, to the level it would have reached without the buydown.

Although a buydown is not a loan in itself, it may be used in combination with many different types of loans, from fixed-rate to adjustable, from conventional to government-backed. Most lenders offer a variety of buydown choices and an impressive assortment of loans to use them with. The result is a loan that's personally designed for you. Ask your real estate agent and loan officer to help tailor a loan that meets your specific needs.

How much will it cost? Because the costs of both types of buydowns are calculated differently, we'll take a closer look at each.

Permanent Buydowns
You would expect a 1% permanent buydown on a 30-year loan to be more expensive than a 1% temporary buydown lasting only three years. It is, but certainly not ten times the cost even though it has ten times the duration.

Calculating A Permanent Buydown Fee: The Lender's Way
Both buydowns are a form of prepaid interest. In each case the lender calculates the amount of interest the borrower would have paid without the buydown, and subtracts the interest paid with the buydown. However this is not the actual cost of the buydown. Since the lender is going to collect the money up front and invest it, he will be earning money on that investment. Therefore it is not necessary to collect the entire interest difference in cash at closing. The lender will use a

'yield chart' to determine how much money, when invested, will yield the amount of interest 'lost' by the buydown.

Calculating A Permanent Buydown Fee: The Easy Way
There's an easier way, thank heavens! The thought of calculations with a yield chart is enough to convince most borrowers that they didn't want a buydown after all. So here is a handy rule of thumb that will give you an estimate of the cost:

For permanent buydowns, estimate a fee of approximately 6% of the loan amount for each 1% reduction in the interest rate.

For example, the fee to buy down the interest rate on a $65,000 loan from 13% to 12% for the entire term of the loan would cost approximately 6% of $65,000, or $3,900:

$$\begin{array}{r} \$65,000 \\ \underline{\times\ .06} \\ \$\ 3,900 \end{array}$$

The cost of buying down the interest rate on that same loan from 13% to 11% (a 2% reduction) would be twice the fee for a 1% permanent buydown, or 12% of the loan amount. On the $65,000 loan, that would amount to $7,800. Similarly, a 3% permanent buydown would be three times the cost of the 1%, and so on. Although the expense involved will set a limit on the size of the buydown, some loans have additional restrictions. Check with your loan officer to see which loans are eligible for the size of permanent buydown you want.

Permanent Buydown With An Adjustable-Rate Loan
Some lenders do not offer permanent buydowns with adjustable-rate loans. In fact, the terms 'permanent' and 'adjustable' may seem contradictory. But one fixed facet of an adjustable-rate loan is the margin.

Adjustable-rate loans have interest rates that adjust or change according to a specific index, such as the 1-year treasury security index. On an adjustable-rate loan with a margin of 2.75, for example, the interest rate will

39

be 2.75% higher than the index rate. It is possible, with a permanent buydown, to reduce the margin. While the interest rate will still change as the index changes, a 1% permanent buydown would mean that the borrower will always pay 1% less than he would have without the buydown. In our example, the margin would be reduced to 1.75%.

The cost of a permanent buydown on an adjustable-rate loan is calculated by the same method we used for the fixed-rate loan. For each 1% reduction in the margin, estimate a fee equal to 6% of the loan amount. In other words, on our $65,000 loan, the cost of a 1% permanent buydown will be approximately $3900, whether the loan is fixed-rate or adjustable-rate.

Temporary Buydowns
Temporary buydowns come in very handy when a borrower can't quite qualify for the loan. A short-term reduction in the interest rate, plus the lower monthly payments that go along, will often lower the amount of income needed to qualify for the loan. But be aware that this is not true for all buydowns. In some cases, the lender will use the pre-buydown rate to qualify the borrower, so be sure to inquire.

Most temporary buydowns last only a few years; some are as short as one year. One-, two-, or three-year buydowns are the most commonly found.

There is plenty of choice in interest rates, too. Temporary buydowns may lower the rate in one of two ways. For a flat rate temporary buydown, the interest rate when lowered stays the same throughout the buydown period. With a graduated temporary buydown, the interest rate starts low and gradually increases until it is back up to the pre-buydown level. We'll study each type separately.

Calculating The Temporary Buydown Fee: Flat Rate
A flat rate temporary buydown works like this: a 2% 3-year buydown on a 13% fixed-rate loan will lower the interest rate to 11% for the first three years. From then on, the rate will stay at 13%.

On an adjustable-rate loan, the length of a temporary buydown usually may not be longer than the period of adjustment. For example, if a loan adjusts every two years, then a one- or two-year buydown may be possible.

To calculate the cost of a temporary flat rate buydown, simply add up the interest that will not be paid as a result of the lower rate. That will be a reasonably close estimate of the buydown fee. Here is an example using a $65,000 loan at 13%, with a 2% buydown for 2 years. Using the amortization chart at the end of the book, determine what the monthly payment would be at 13% and, with the buydown, at 11%, then subtract.

	Loan Amount	Interest Rate	Monthly Payment
Without buydown	$65,000	13%	$718.90
With buydown	$65,000	11%	$618.80
Subtract to find the difference:			$100.10

That difference, $100.10, is the extra monthly interest that would be "saved" with the buydown. If we multiply it by the number of months the buydown remains in effect, we get the approximate cost of the buydown. Since our example is a two-year buydown, we will multiply $100.10 by 24. This buydown will cost $2402.40.

Calculating The Temporary Buydown Fee: Graduated Rate
Graduated Buydowns have interest rates that start low and gradually increase until they reach the pre-buydown rate. There are a number of different interest rate combinations possible. The most common graduated buydown is known as the 3-2-1. The interest rate is reduced 3% the first year, 2% the second and 1% the third. From the fourth year on, it remains at the regular pre-buydown rate.

Other buydown combinations are the 3-3-1, the 3-1-1, the 3-1, the 2-2-1, the 2-1-1 and the 2-1. Many lenders allow borrowers to design buydowns that meet their needs; other lenders offer only certain combinations.

41

There may be restrictions on the size, the length or the pattern of graduated buydowns, and these will vary from lender to lender.

If you thoroughly enjoy math, the fee for a graduated buydown may be calculated the same way we estimated a flat rate buydown. Be sure to figure the cost of each interest step separately, then add your answers to give you the grand total.

But again, there's an easier way. Use this handy chart to give you the approximate cost of a graduated buydown, keeping in mind that fees sometimes vary slightly from lender to lender.

Cost Of A Graduated Buydown

Type of Buydown	Estimated Buydown Fee
3-2-1	.055 X the amount of the loan
3-3-1	.064 X the amount of the loan
3-1-1	.046 X the amount of the loan
3-1	.037 X the amount of the loan
2-2-1	.046 X the amount of the loan
2-1-1	.037 X the amount of the loan
2-1	.028 X the amount of the loan

Using the chart, we can calculate the cost of a 3-2-1 buydown for a $65,000 loan:

$$\begin{array}{r} \$65{,}000 \\ \underline{\text{x } .055} \\ \$ \ 3{,}575 \end{array}$$

Discount Points: A "Hidden" Buydown
Discount points were once used primarily with FHA and VA loans but today are a common facet of conventional loans. They are a form of prepaid interest, charged by the lender at closing. Each point costs 1% of the loan amount. By paying the cost of the discount points, a borrower effectively reduces the interest rate on the loan. (Either the seller or the buyer may pay the discount fee.) A lender, for example, may offer one 30-year fixed-rate loan at 12.5% interest, a 3% loan fee and no discount points. A similar loan from the same lender might be available at 12% interest, with the same

3% loan fee but 3 discount points, in addition to the fee. The payment of the points will reduce the interest rate in this case by one half of 1%.

Many borrowers are not aware that this is actually a form of permanent buydown. The words "buydown fee" or "discount points" may not actually be used. Often the cost of the points is added to the loan fee quoted by a lender. If a loan officer mentions a fee of 6% and loan fees offered by other lenders are 2% or 3%, it probably includes discount points to provide an attractive rate.

ADVANTAGES OF A BUYDOWN

1. Lower monthly payments, initially or for the term of the loan.
2. Lower income needed to qualify for the loan. (Often true but not always the case.)
3. Borrower may often obtain a larger loan. Buyer may afford a more expensive home.
4. Relatives, friends or the seller may often pay all or part of the fee, reducing the borrower's expense.
5. Increased saleability when seller offers a buydown.

DISADVANTAGE OF A BUYDOWN

1. The only disadvantage of a buydown is its cost, which must be paid in cash at closing.

CHAPTER 6

Graduated-Payment Loans (GPMS)

DEFINITION: **A Graduated-Payment Mortgage Loan is a fixed-rate loan which has monthly payments that start at a lower-than-normal level and increase at specified intervals during the first few years of the loan. The purpose is to create a loan that is affordable.**

If you want a true conventional GPM in Oregon, you are in for a difficult search. At this time, I do not know of a lender who is offering this loan, yet it is touted in national magazines and deserves to be mentioned here.

Government loans are a different matter. Later in this book I will discuss the FHA Section 245 loan program, the quintessential GPM. The Veterans Administration also offers a graduated payment plan. Both are similar to the standard GPM described here.

How A GPM Works
At first glance, a graduated-payment loan looks like a graduated buydown. There are the same low initial payments and the same gradual payment increases. What is missing in the GPM is the buydown fee. Then is this simply a free buydown? Not at all. While a buydown is paid for up front, at closing, the GPM is paid for during the term of the loan.

Let's take a closer look at the GPM. As you can see from the chart, the initial payments are much lower than those on a standard fixed-rate level-payment loan. In fact they are too low to cover all of the interest that is due, and of course, that means that there is nothing left over to apply to the principal. Therefore, the

45

principal is not reduced, and we are also faced with the problem of unpaid interest. (The buydown fee would have covered in advance the cost of any unpaid interest.)

------- a graduated-payment loan with five annual increases
--- ------ a standard 30-year level-payment loan

0 1 2 3 4 5 ..... 30 years YEARS

THE GRADUATED-PAYMENT LOAN

Deferred Interest

Lenders customarily defer the interest payment, adding it to the loan balance, where it will be paid over the term of the loan. This deferred interest, or "negative amortization" as it is often called, is one reason why financing fashion has turned away from graduated-payment loans. At times when property values are falling, deferred interest can be a problem. Borrowers have discovered that their loan balance, padded with the deferred interest, could exceed the market value of the home. It is hard to find a buyer for a $60,000 home financed by a $63,000 loan which must be assumed or repaid in full.

Note that the final level of monthly payments is higher than that for the standard level-payment loan. This is a result of two things: the higher loan balance, thanks to the deferred interest, and the shorter term at the time of the last increase. At each increase the payments are amortized over the remaining term of the loan; shorter terms bring higher monthly payments.

To avoid deferred interest, lenders prefer to use buydowns to provide the graduated-payment feature. Even though there are higher closing costs to face with a buydown fee, the safety factor may be well worth the price.

ADVANTAGES OF A GRADUATED-PAYMENT MORTGAGE LOAN

1. Low initial monthly payments make qualifying easier. (Less income will be required.)
2. Borrowers can qualify for a larger GPM than for a standard fixed-rate level-payment loan.
3. Interest rate is fixed.

DISADVANTAGES OF A GRADUATED-PAYMENT MORTGAGE LOAN

1. Negative amortization (deferred interest) will increase the loan balance.
2. Higher final monthly payments, as compared to standard fixed-rate level-payment loans.

CHAPTER 7

Loans With Calls

DEFINITION: **Loans which give the lender the right to "call" the loan (demand payment in full) on a specified date.**

A loan with a call provision is similar to a contract with a balloon payment. Both must be paid off at a certain date agreed to by the borrower at the time the loan is made. Sometimes the lender will offer to extend the due date, perhaps with an interest rate increase and/or a servicing fee. Whether or not an extension is possible depends upon the wording of the original agreement and the lender's current policies.

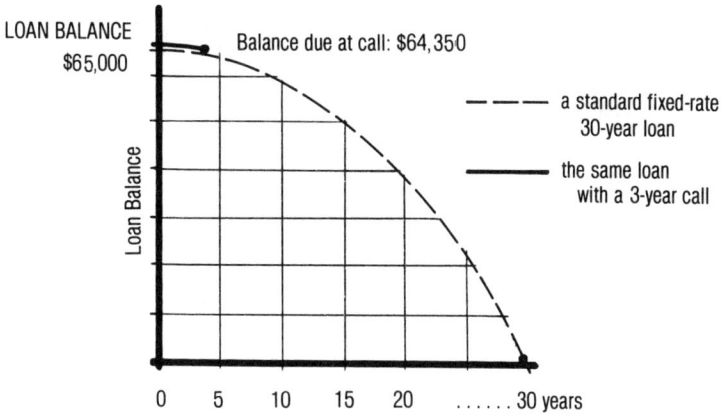

LOAN BALANCE
$65,000

Balance due at call: $64,350

Loan Balance

— — — a standard fixed-rate
30-year loan

———— the same loan
with a 3-year call

0   5   10   15   20   . . . . . . 30 years

A LOAN WITH A CALL

Comparing Loan With And Without Calls

Let's compare two $65,000 fixed rate loans with payments amortized over 30 years. The interest rate on each is 13%. One is a standard fixed rate 30-year loan that will be paid off in 30 years. The second is an identical loan except that it has a 3-year call. Notice how much of the original loan amount remains to be paid at the end of three years.

49

Calls Don't Win Popularity Contests

Loans with calls are risky business. Do not consider them unless you are absolutely certain that you will be able to pay off the loan when due. During the early years of the loan, most of each payment is the interest that is due. Very little is credited toward the principal. At the end of the first few years, the loan balance is still uncomfortably close to the starting figure.

Lenders understand the risks, too, and that is why many do not offer this type of loan. In most cases, it is not profitable for lenders to foreclose and they avoid making loans that have a chance of turning sour. But even the best-laid plans run into problems, as Julie and Ed Putnam discovered.

Case History: The Putnams

Julie and Ed did not spend enough research time when they bought a home in Oregon. The loan they chose had a 3-year call. In return for the added risk, the Putnams saved a half percentage point of interest, lowering their monthly payments by $70 a month. That would add up to a savings of $1600 over the 3-year period.

As the Putnams calculated it, the "added risk" wasn't much risk at all to them. They bought the home as a temporary stop, en route to buying a farm within a year. As soon as they found the farm, they would sell the house and move. That certainly would be well before the call date.

Yet three years later, Julie and Ed were still in the "temporary" home. Oh yes, they found a farm, but they couldn't finance it without first selling the house. Even the most creative financing techniques did not help. The Putnams needed a quick sale.

Finding a buyer for the home was not an easy job, especially since Julie and Ed needed to recoup every penny of their equity in order to buy the farm. Since the loan on the house had a call provision, buyers shied away. New financing was required and rates were high. By choosing temporary financing for their temporary home, the Putnams had backed themselves into a corner.

Julie and Ed had to postpone buying a farm. They refinanced their home, spending over $2500 in loan fees and closing costs. That cancelled out the $1600 interest benefit the original loan had given them. Even if they had originally financed their home with a fully amortized loan, (a 30-year loan) they might still have been unable to buy the farm. But knowing that they would want to sell the home in a few years, they would have been wise to make sure that their loan did not discourage a sale.

Assumability of Loans With Calls
As with other types of financing, some loans with calls are assumable, some are not. In the example above, the Putnam's loan could not be assumed. Even if the lender had allowed an assumption, the three-year call would have been unattractive to a buyer.

Some loans with calls have a dual assumption policy. In a recent transaction for a client of mine, the loan in question had a seven-year call. Since the loan was already six-and-one-half years old, the due date was close. The new buyer had a choice: for an assumption fee of 1% of the loan balance, the loan could be assumed for the remaining few months only; or for a 2% fee, the loan could be extended for an additional 23 years. In either case, the interest would be increased by 2%. Could that even be called a choice? Of course the buyer took the second route.

When you apply for a loan, ask specific questions about its assumability. Keep in mind that a loan that is not assumable or one that is assumable but still subject to the call provision could make resale more difficult. You could be forced to refinance the home, as the Putnams were, losing several hundred or thousands of dollars in the process.

ADVANTAGES OF A LOAN WITH A CALL

1. Some lenders offer a small reduction in interest rate (as compared to a fixed-rate 30-year loan).
2. The slightly lower interest rate would require a lower income to qualify for the loan.

DISADVANTAGES OF A LOAN WITH A CALL

1. If you are not able to sell the home before the loan is called, you must come up with sufficient cash to pay off the loan. You may not be able to get a new loan when you need it.
2. Interest savings will be offset by expensive refinancing costs and possibly a higher interest rate on the new loan.
3. This loan usually does not offer sufficient benefits to cover the risk. If a lower interest rate or lower income requirement is your goal, there are safer ways to finance your home. Read on!

CHAPTER 8

Growing-Equity
Mortgage Loans (GEMs)

DEFINITION: **A Growing Equity Mortgage Loan is a fixed-rate loan with monthly payments that increase at regular intervals, to result in an early payoff.**

A GEM loan is an interesting combination of the loans we have studied so far: fixed-rate short- and long-term loans, plus graduated-payment loans. Like the 15-year loan, it has early payoff as its goal. Most GEMs are repaid within 12 to 17 years. And yet, like the GPM, it has payments that increase regularly.

How A GEM Works
Let's use as an example, our $65,000 fixed-rate loan at 13% interest. As we have seen in previous chapters, for a 30-year term, the monthly payment would be $719. If we wanted to pay off the loan in a hurry, we could opt for the 15-year term, but that would increase our monthly payments to $822 (or perhaps $801, if the lender were to give us a ½% interest break).

However, the higher monthly payments on the 15-year term also mean a higher monthly income needed to qualify for the loan. That stops many would-be borrowers in their tracks. To the rescue, comes the GEM. Since the initial payment on a GEM is the same as that of the 30-year loan, or even lower, qualifying for the GEM is no more difficult.

In our example, the monthly payments would be $719 a month for the first year. From there on, the amount of the increase depends upon which particular GEM we select, and lenders offer a wide assortment to choose from. For instance, one GEM has payment increases

of 3% per year for 15 years. Another calls for 5½%
increase per year through year 5, with level payments
from year 6 on. Both loans will be paid off in less than
15 years.

Comparing GEMs and Fixed Payment Loans

Let's compare these three $65,000 fixed-rate loans at
13% interest: the standard 30-year loan and the two
GEMs mentioned above. All three will start with
payments of $719 per month. Notice the payment
range for each. Some borrowers would feel more
comfortable with the gradual 3% increase over the life
of the loan, while others would prefer a rapid rise in the
early years and level payments after that.

——————— GEM w/3% increases per year
— · — ·· GEM w/5 5½% increases
—— —— standard 30-year loan

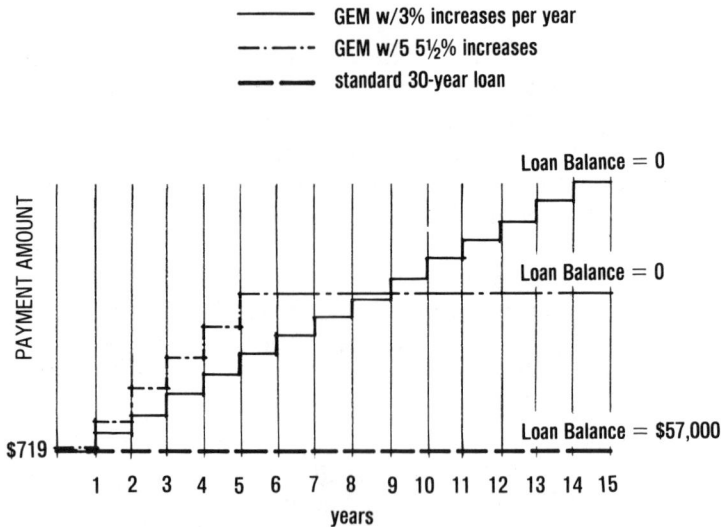

COMPARING GEMS AND LEVEL-PAYMENT LOAN

As you can see, at the end of the fifteenth year, the
GEM loans have been repaid, while the balance due on
the 30-year loan is still a whopping $57,000. It is
important to note that all three are fixed rate loans at
the same interest rate. The actual interest paid the first
year is the same for all three loans. However, by
increasing the amount of the monthly payment on the
GEMs, we are increasing the amount that is applied
toward the principal each month. Therefore the loan
balance is reduced at a much faster rate, and so less
interest is due on the GEMs from the second year on.

The Threat Of Deferred Interest (Negative Amortization)
As explained in the chapter on Graduated-Payment Mortgage loans, deferred interest is interest that is not paid when due but added to the loan balance instead. This occurs only when the monthly payment is not sufficiently large to cover the cost of the interest.

In the two GEM loans we charted above, the initial monthly payments are similar to the standard 30-year loan payments. That amount will amply cover the interest that is due, and so there will be no deferred interest in either case.

However, many lenders offer borrowers an affordable feature: they design their GEMs with very low monthly payments the first few years. While this does help more people qualify for the loan, borrowers should be aware that the loan balance will increase each month interest is deferred. If housing prices should tumble drastically, a homeowner who has deferred interest could find that the loan balance exceeds the value of the home.

How Much Interest Is Due?
To find the amount of interest that is owed in any month, multiply the current loan balance by the interest rate, then divide by 12. For our $65,000 loan at 13%, the calculations are:

$$\frac{\$65,000 \times .13}{12} = \frac{8450}{12} = \$704.16$$

For any type of loan with a balance of $65,000 and an interest rate of 13%, the amount of interest due that month is $704.16. Therefore, any loan that calls for a payment of less than that will have deferred interest. If the monthly payment is more than $704.16, the difference will be credited to the principal, and the loan balance will decrease.

Buydowns With GEM Loans
Some lenders not only offer, but also encourage buydowns on GEMs to avoid the problem of deferred interest. A buydown payment equal to the deferred interest (or part of it), will give the borrower the benefit of lower initial monthly payments and ease of qualifying but will eliminate the increase in the loan balance.

Who Should Consider A GEM?
GEMs are for borrowers who are absolutely certain that their income will increase in pace with the rising monthly payments. Some plans have moderate increases over the life of the loan, perhaps a $400 difference between year one and year 15 on a $65,000 loan. Others, with very low initial payments, may have a $1,000 spread. Remember that the main purpose of a GEM is the early payoff, not necessarily affordability.

Assumability Of A GEM
Many GEMs are assumable but, as with other loans, most lenders today reserve the right to raise the interest rate and approve the buyer. GEMs are less easily assumed, or perhaps it would be more accurate to say that there are fewer people who are able to assume a GEM, as compared to a fixed rate 30-year loan. First, the monthly payments will be higher and would-be buyers may not qualify for the assumption.

Second, the owner's equity increases at a rapid rate, so that the difference between the sales price and the loan balance will be greater with the GEM. If the seller is not willing to carry a second mortgage, or if the lender forbids it, the buyer must come up with that difference in cash.

ADVANTAGES OF A GEM
1. Rapid equity buildup. The home is owned free and clear within 12 to 17 years.
2. There is a remarkable savings in interest, when compared to a 30-year loan.
3. The interest rate is fixed.
4. The payments are predictable.

DISADVANTAGES OF A GEM
1. Within a few years, payments are considerably higher than loans with fixed payment amounts.
2. Some GEMs have deferred interest that increases the loan balance.
3. Fewer buyers are able to assume a GEM, thereby reducing the saleability of the home.

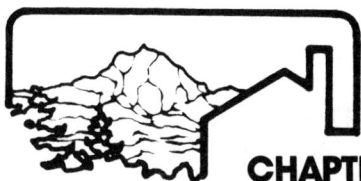

CHAPTER 9

Adjustable-Rate Mortgage Loans (ARMs)

DEFINITION: An Adjustable-Rate Mortgage Loan has an interest rate that fluctuates according to a specified index. The rate is adjusted, and corresponding changes are made in the monthly payments, at prearranged intervals over the life of the loan.

Adjustable-Rate Mortgage Loans were introduced in the early 1980s, with the hope that they would solve many of the problems that had troubled both lenders and homebuyers. Since the interest rate on an ARM was designed to "go with the flow", lenders would no longer be stuck holding unprofitable low-interest loans. Here was their chance to rewrite the rules for the no-win financing game our interest-wild, deregulated society had organized.

Homebuyers needed help, too. With interest rates reaching frightening heights, who could qualify for a loan large enough to buy a home? Not many. If few could buy, few could sell; many owners were forced to lower their asking price just to find a buyer who could afford the financing.

Adjustable-rate loans solve both problems. Because the lender does not have to bear the entire loss in interest if rates rise, he can afford to be generous. Borrowers willing to share the risk, by accepting an ARM, will be offered an interest rate that is significantly lower than the rate for a fixed-rate loan. The lower rate produces smaller initial monthly payments and these, in turn, make qualifying easier.

How An ARM Works

All adjustable-rate mortgages have four factors in common:

1. **Period of Adjustment:** This tells how frequently the interest rate will be adjusted. For example, with a 1-year ARM, the interest rate will be adjusted each year. The most common are the 1-, 3-, and 5-year ARMs.

2. **Note Rate:** This is the initial interest rate the lender will charge for the first period of adjustment. The shorter the period of adjustment, the lower the note rate. (If it is more than 2% lower than the interest on a fixed rate 30-year loan, be wary. This may, in fact, be a graduated-payment ARM which will be covered in the next chapter.)

3. **Index:** This is the guideline that is used as the basis for adjustment. If the index rate has increased at the time of adjustment, the interest rate on the ARM will be raised accordingly. Different indexes are used, a common one being the index of U.S. Treasury Bills.

4. **Margin:** This amount is added to the index rate to establish the interest rate on an ARM. For example, if the index on an ARM is the 1-year T-Bill rate, and that happens to be at 9.24% at the time of adjustment, the new interest rate would be 9.24% plus the margin. If the margin is 2.65%, the new rate would be 9.24% + 2.65% or 11.89%.

This chart shows how the interest rate on an ARM is adjusted. Notice that fluctuations in the index only affect the ARM's rate at the time of adjustment.

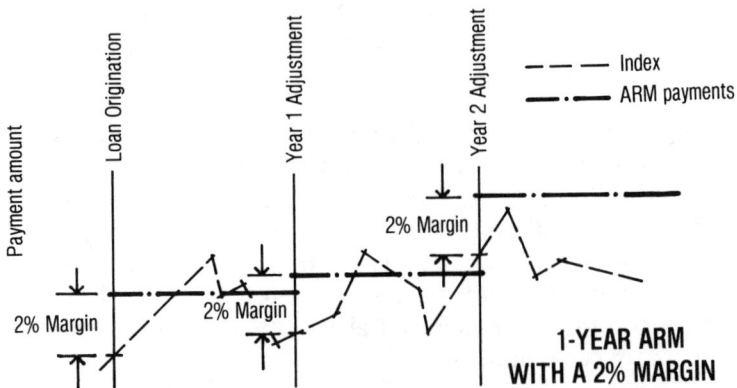

1-YEAR ARM
WITH A 2% MARGIN

58

Safety Devices Mean Sharing The Risk
The first ARMs through the starting gate were un-controlled beasts that made potential borrowers very nervous. What would happen if the index took a flying leap, 10 points higher? On some loans, the borrower was stuck with outrageously high payments and suffered from what is known as "payment shock". The lender sat back and counted the profits, or instituted foreclosure proceedings against the unfortunate gambler.

Today's ARMs are tame by comparison. Safety features have been added to protect the consumer and to avoid a fatal case of payment shock. Although the index still fluctuates, its effect on the new ARMs can be limited. Here are some safety features to shop for in an ARM:

1. **Lifetime Cap:** This is the maximum percentage of interest increase or decrease that may occur during the term of the loan. For instance, a 5% lifetime cap on a 10.75% ARM means that the interest may never exceed 15.75% or be less than 5.75%.
2. **Adjustment Cap:** This is the maximum percentage of interest increase or decrease that may occur at the time of adjustment. On 1-year ARMs, it is often called the Annual Cap. A 10.75% ARM with a 2% adjustment cap may be increased to no more than 12.75% on its first adjustment. On each succeeding adjustment, an additional 2% may be added. Decreases work in the same way.
3. **Payment Cap:** This is an option that has been available on some ARMs, but fortunately is fading from sight these days. It limits the increase in payment amount when the rate is adjusted. For example, on an ARM with monthly payments of $700, a 7.5% payment cap would prevent the pay-ment from exceeding $752.50 at the first adjustment, no matter how high the index has climbed. But watch out! If you are limiting the payment amount but not the interest rate, your payment may not be large enough to cover the interest that is due. The unpaid (deferred) interest may be added to your loan balance. (Read more about deferred interest in the chapters on Growing Equity Mortgage Loans and Graduated-Payment ARMs.)

Amortization Of An ARM

Most ARMs have a 30-year term. In other words, their initial payments are amortized over 30 years. Each time the interest rate on an ARM is adjusted, the payments are recalculated and re-amortized over the remaining term.

For example, on a 3-year ARM, at the first adjustment there will be 27 years remaining. Therefore, to calculate the new payment amount with an amortization chart (Appendix I), use the new interest rate, the remaining loan balance, and a 27-year term.

Shopping For An ARM

It is not as easy to shop for an adjustable-rate loan as it is for a standard fixed-rate loan because there are so many variables to consider. Each lender may offer several ARMs with different adjustment periods, note rates, margins, indexes, and caps. In addition, there are some other features, such as convertibility and assumability, to investigate. You may find it easier to plot a hypothetical case for each loan. Which would suit your needs better? What would happen to each if the index rose? Your loan officer has followed the path of the ARMs and can help you understand the limits of risk or reward with each of his or her loans.

Which Index Is Best?

Even after long research, I can't answer that question. All the indexes fluctuate, of course, in concert with the economic picture. A lender may have three different 1-year ARMs, each based upon a different index.

To make matters even worse for the bewildered borrower, some of these have names that don't exactly roll off the tip of one's tongue. Most of us have heard of T-Bills; those are a very common index. Many lenders use the U.S. Treasury Securities, a broader-based index. Then there's the Cost of Funds Index, not widely used in Oregon at the moment. Finally, you might encounter the tongue-twister of them all, guaranteed to leave even stout-hearted borrowers gasping: the 'Federal Home Loan Mortgage Corporation posted yield requirement for 60-day delivery of fixed-rate 30-year loans plus 50 basis points' index!

Fortunately, the two most common indexes, Treasury Bills and Securities are also the best known. No matter what the index, your loan officer should be able to provide you with a history of its meanderings. If you have narrowed your choice down to loans based on two different indexes, study a graph of each to see how its volatility would affect your interest rate.

Convertibility To A Fixed Rate Loan
Many ARMs have a provision that allows the borrower to convert the ARM to a fixed-rate loan at a later date. This is a handy feature to have if interest rates decline. Here again, there is a vast difference in policies. With some ARMs, conversion is possible only at specified times, for example, at the time of loan adjustment. Other ARMs permit conversion on any banking day during the first five years.

Some lenders charge a nominal fee, or no fee at all for converting. Others charge a hefty loan fee. Be sure to ask about these details and inquire whether or not they are subject to change before your ARM is converted.

Buydowns With An ARM
Both permanent and temporary buydowns are available for adjustable-rate loans, although temporary buydowns are far more common. Not every ARM has this option, so be sure to check with your loan officer to see which loans offer it.

Buydowns make ARMs even more affordable by reducing the monthly payments on a permanent or temporary basis. That, in turn, often makes it easier for the borrower to qualify for the loan. This offers the same result as the Graduated-Payment ARM (discussed in the next chapter) but without the problem of deferred interest. Refer to the chapter on Buydowns to learn how to calculate the fee.

Assumability Of An ARM
Lenders are more likely to permit a buyer to assume an ARM than a fixed-rate 30-year loan. The reason is, of course, that the ARMs are more profitable for a lender

since they keep pace with the economy. But that does not mean that all ARMs are assumable, and those that are usually have strings attached.

For example, it is not uncommon for the lender to retain the right to adjust the interest rate at the time of assumption, even if the next official adjustment date is years away. That may make the assumption less attractive than a new loan with a buydown or graduated-payment feature. As in other assumptions, the new buyer will usually be required to qualify for the loan, based upon the new rate and payments.

While ARMs are becoming more and more acceptable to the general public, prospective buyers who are searching for the perfect assumption would much prefer to assume a fixed-rate loan. This may change as ARMs reach a graceful middle age and buyers find that there are fewer fixed-rate assumptions available.

Case History: The Randalls And The McCalls
Here are two families who chose adjustable-rate mortgages, but for different reasons. Each originally wanted a fixed-rate 30-year loan. After all, they had always had fixed-rate loans, so why shouldn't they continue the trend?

The Randalls knew when they arrived that their stay in Oregon would be a short one, eighteen months to two years at most. Monte Randall would then be transferred back to company head-quarters in Minnesota. His employer was among that vanishing breed of companies able and willing to buy the Randall home when the transfer occurred. The Randalls would receive their equity in cash and the company would handle the sale of the home. Therefore assumability wasn't of any import-ance in the choice of a loan.

At the time the Randalls came in to make loan application, the interest rate on a fixed-rate 30-year loan was 13.75%. They gulped. Their last loan had been at 8%. When the loan officer suggested a 3-year ARM at 12.25%, the Randalls said, "Absolutely Not!". But when the loan officer pointed out that the interest savings with the ARM would amount to $105 a month, or over $2500 during the two-year period, the Randalls looked intrigued. After all, why pay more than necessary? Their accountant concurred. The Randalls would be back in Minnesota before their loan had a chance to readjust.

The McCalls chose an ARM for another reason. They went house-hunting with their agent and decided that a splendid riverfront villa was the only home they could ever love. One problem: it was just a tad too expensive even with the seller's final price reduction.

Although the McCalls were reluctant to consider anything but a fixed-rate loan, they found that their income was not high enough for them to qualify for it. A buydown would have solved the problem but neither the buyers nor the seller had the available cash, and no fairy godmother appeared to save the day.

So the McCalls were forced to consider an ARM. When they sat down to study it, they found that it was confusing at first but not quite the ogre they thought it was. In fact, the ARM they finally chose was quite manageable for them. Thier income was sufficient to qualify, their payments would stay level for one year, and after that, their expected pay increases could easily keep pace with the worst possible scenario of rate hikes. In short, it was an excellent choice for them.

ADVANTAGES OF AN ARM
1. Lower interest rate (at least initially) than that for a fixed-rate loan.
2. Lower monthly payments initially.
3. Lower income needed to qualify.
4. If interest rates decline, so will an ARM's rate.

DISADVANTAGES OF AN ARM
1. Unpredictability of interest rate and payments.

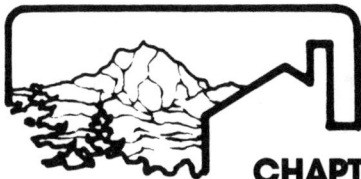

CHAPTER 10

Graduated-Payment ARMs (GPARMs)

DEFINITION: **A Graduated-Payment Adjustable-Rate Mortgage Loan is a standard ARM with monthly payments that start at a lower level and gradually increase during the early years of the loan.**

Graduated-Payment ARMs are masters at traveling incognito. Many lenders simply leave off the letters "GP" and lump them together in their loan rosters with standard ARMs. It is important, however, to be aware of their differences.

A GPARM is a complex loan, by far the most difficult for borrowers to understand. It is the only loan with both graduated payments and an adjustable interest that can also affect the monthly payments.

With the ARMs we discussed in the last chapter, the first monthly payment is determined by the note rate, which is the "jumping off" point for the interest on the loan. A GPARM has a note rate, too. This is the true interest rate on the loan (at least for the first period) and is the actual amount of interest that must be paid.

But a GPARM has a second rate, not found in a standard ARM. This is sometimes known as the Initial Payment Calculation Rate or the Introductory Rate and it will be lower than the note rate.

This lower rate is used to determine the first level of monthly payments. It has nothing whatsoever to do with the actual interest that is due; that is based on the higher note rate. The introductory rate is an arbitrary level chosen by the underwriter of the loan. Since it is lower than the note rate, a payment based on the introductory rate will be lower than a payment based on a note rate.

Accentuate The Positive . . .
That means that the initial monthly payments on a GPARM will be smaller than those on a standard ARM at the same note rate. That also means that less income will be required to qualify for a GPARM, if the lender is willing to qualify the borrower at the lower rate. Be sure to ask your loan officer which rate will be used, since rules vary from loan to loan.

But Be Aware Of The Negative
All of this good news may overshadow the one drawback to a GPARM: deferred interest, otherwise known as negative amortization. If you have read the chapter on GPM loans, you'll remember that deferred interest is interest that is due but not paid. Instead, it is added to the loan balance.

Deferred interest occurs when the monthly payment is too small to cover the entire amount of interest due. In a GPARM, it is a fact of life. The extent of the deferred interest depends upon two things: how much of a difference there is between the introductory rate and the note rate, and how quickly the graduated payments catch up to those of a standard ARM. The larger the difference and the slower the catching up, the greater the deferred interest will be.

So What's Wrong With Deferred Interest?
I have two objections to deferred interest. First, the loan balance is increased by the amount of the deferred interest. In a normal market, the owner's equity would be in no danger. But when housing prices are falling, deferred interest increases the owner's chance of having a loan balance greater than the value of the home. That is known as "equity shock". If the owner should have to sell the home at that time, the lender must be paid the full amount of the loan, even though the actual sales price is lower.

My second objection is that the borrower ends up paying interest on the deferred interest, when it becomes part of the loan balance. For this reason, the total amount of interest paid on a GPARM is greater than that on an ARM.

Yet there are many times when a home could not be financed without this type of loan. If the borrower is aware of the risks and feels they are manageable, a GPARM might be a good choice.

Catching Up To An ARM
GPARM loans have payment plans to increase the monthly payments on a regular basis. For example, one plan calls for a 7½% payment increase each year until the loan is on a fully amortized basis. That is, until the monthly payment is large enough to include both principal and interest. Of course, at the same time the GPARM is subject to regularly scheduled rate increases. This would create a whopping jump in payments if the loan does not also include a payment cap.

ADVANTAGES OF A GPARM
1. Lower initial monthly payments than either an ARM or a fixed-rate 30-year loan.
2. Usually the easiest loan to qualify for.
3. Lower interest rate than for a fixed-rate loan.
4. If interest rates decline, so will a GPARM's.

DISADVANTAGES OF A GPARM
1. Interest rates and payments are unpredictable.
2. Negative amortization increases the loan balance.
3. More interest paid over the life of the loan (as compared to an ARM).

CHAPTER 11

Federal Land Bank Loans

DEFINITION: The Federal Land Bank (also known as Farm Credit Service) offers variable interest rate conventional loans for rural residences and farms only.

Up to now, the conventional loans we have discussed have been specific types of loans available from many sources, both institutional and private. Federal Land Bank Loans, on the other hand, may be obtained only through a branch of the Land Bank itself.

This national lending institution was established in 1916, with seed money from the Federal Government. That money has long since been repaid and the Land Bank is a thriving conventional lender providing long-term loans in rural areas.

It is a unique organization for three reasons. First, the Land Bank is a cooperative, owned by its borrowers, who invest in the bank as a loan requirement. Second, it makes long-term real estate loans only; it does not offer the other services we expect of a bank, such as checking and savings accounts. Finally, it is limited by law to serving rural areas; small towns, rural subdivisions and farms. Financing funds are obtained from the sale of bonds.

Two Kinds Of Loans
The Land Bank offers only two types of loans. One is for rural residences, the other for part- or full-time farms.

Certain features are true of both. The interest rate on all Land Bank loans is variable; it may be adjusted up or down throughout the term of the loan. It has, however, been relatively stable in recent years, and is comparable to the rates charged by other institutions. Borrowers are notified 30 days in advance of a rate and payment increase.

For Rural Residence loans and Part-time Farm loans, a buyer's down payment or equity must be at least 35% or 40% of the value of the property. For Full-time Farm loans, a smaller down payment, a minimum of 15% of the value, may be allowed. Each situation is judged on an individual basis by the loan officer. Loans are available for refinancing property as long as the new Land Bank loan is in first lien position. In other words, Land Bank does not offer second mortgage loans.

Land Bank Is Owned By The Borrowers
Each borrower is required to invest 5% of the loan amount in Land Bank stock. It may either be paid in cash or borrowed in addition to the loan. When the loan balance has dwindled so that it is equal to the amount of the investment, the invested cash is used to pay off the loan.

Assuming A Land Bank Loan
Assumption of a Land Bank loan is permitted. However the new buyer must qualify for the loan. If the seller or another lender carries a second mortgage, the cost of the monthly payment on it is added to the monthly payment on the Land Bank loan and this figure is used to qualify the buyer. Assumption fees are currently $100.

Rural Residence Loans
If the property to be financed is a year-round, owner occupied home on less than five acres of tillable land in a rural area, it may be a candidate for a rural residence loan. The value of the home plus land may not exceed $90,000. (If it does, it may be eligible for a farm loan, which has no ceiling.) In addition, the home must be in modern condition, with all utilities, dependable water and sewage systems, and a year-round road.

The Land Bank will finance a home to be constructed, if the borrower has a firm bid from a contractor and a workman-like set of plans. No do-it-yourself projects are acceptable.

In determining whether or not the potential borrower qualifies for the loan, the Land Bank is more conservative than other conventional lenders. For a Rural Residence loan, the borrower's payment for principal, interest, taxes and insurance may not exceed 25% of the gross family income. Many other lenders use 28%. (Read the chapter on Qualifying For A Loan to learn how to calculate this, but be sure to use the figure of 25% in the First Ratio.)

Farm Loans
Farm Loans are for property that produces an agricultural income. This is how they differ from Rural Residential Loans. Part-time Farms need not be wholly self-supporting but must show farm income that reduces the cost of ownership. For example, keeping two horses on a five-acre tract does not qualify it as a farm, but selling livestock or produce from that same land would make it eligible.

There is no limit on the value of the property, as there is for a Rural Residence Loan. Refinancing and new construction funds are available.

Where To Apply
Loan application must be made at a branch of the Federal Land Bank serving the particular county in which the property is located. There are fourteen branch offices throughout Oregon, in the following cities: Coquille, Harrisburg, Hillsboro, Klamath Falls, La Grande, Medford, Ontario, Oregon City, Pendleton, Redmond, Roseburg, Salem, Tillamook, and The Dalles. Check the telephone directory for the number of the nearest branch.

For further information, contact the head office:
Federal Land Bank of Spokane
Drawer TAF-C4
Spokane, Washington, 99220

There are other farm credit organizations throughout the country, providing financing in rural areas. The Land Bank System is a large nationwide network and for this reason has been included here.

Part III

Government Loans

DEFINITION: A Government Loan is one which is either insured, guaranteed or funded by a department or agency of the government.

Oregonians are fortunate to have a wide choice of government loans available for home financing. First the Federal government offers a splendid banquet of loans through the Department of Housing and Urban Development, the Veterans Administration, and the Department of Agriculture. Then the State of Oregon co-hosts the party, with loans from the Department of Veterans' Affairs and the Department of Commerce. Everyone is invited. Government loans are not just for select minority groups or low-income borrowers. Certainly, some are available only to veterans or first-time buyers or persons with an income below a designated level. But many government loans have no personal restrictions of this type and are offered to any qualified borrower.

Why Choose A Government Loan?
There are many reasons for considering a government loan. First of all, government loans usually have lower interest rates than conventional loans. Since lower rates mean lower monthly payments, it is often easier to qualify for a government loan. In addition, many government loans are available to borrowers with little or no down payment. Another tempting advantage is the lower loan fees on some types of government loans. So before jumping into conventional financing, study the array of government loans to see if one fits your needs.

Where Does The Money Come From?
Government loans are funded in many different ways. Some, such as those offered by the Oregon Department of Veterans' Affairs, are funded directly by the department, through the sale of bonds.

Others are funded by individual lending institutions, with government approval or guidelines, and later purchased by a governmental agency. Some loans are insured or guaranteed by the government against loss to the lender through foreclosure.

In the chapters that follow, we will take a look at the various government loans available to Oregonians.

CHAPTER 12

HUD/FHA Loans

DEFINITION: **The Federal Housing Administration (FHA) offers programs to insure home mortgage loans so that lenders can provide affordable financing at lower-than-conventional interest rates.**

There are more FHA loans made each day than any other type of government loan, yet FHA does not lend a cent. Neither does HUD, the Department of Housing and Urban Development, under which FHA operates. Instead, it provides a mortgage insurance program for institutional lenders. With FHA insurance to protect them, these lenders are willing and able to make higher-risk loans: loans with a higher LTV ratio, lower loan fees and attractive interest rates.

Since 1934 when the National Housing Act established it, FHA has been a leader in innovative home financing. Widespread use of the amortized loan, better home construction methods and the standardization of appraisal techniques are just a few of the results FHA has achieved over the past half century.

The FHA Insurance Program
FHA mortgage insurance directly benefits the lending institutions that provide FHA loans. This insurance protects the lenders against the loss they would incur if foreclosure becomes necessary. Since statistics have shown that the higher the loan-to-value ratio, the greater the likelihood of default, common sense keeps lenders from loaning more than 95% of the value on conventional financing. With the FHA insurance, however, lenders feel safe in going even higher, in accordance with FHA guidelines. For some loans, such as the FHA veterans' loan, this can mean close to 100% LTV financing!

The FHA mortgage insurance program is funded by the borrowers, although sellers may pay the insurance premium if they wish to do so. Mortgage insurance is an unavoidable requirement on all FHA financing. The method of payment varies with the particular type of loan; some FHA loans have a one-time charge, while others have a monthly premium.

Who Is Eligible For A FHA Loan?
Anyone may apply for most FHA loan programs. Rich or less-than-wealthy, U.S. citizen or not, there is a loan available to any person who is a good credit risk and financially able to repay it. Some FHA loan programs, however, are more restrictive. There are loans just for veterans, some for first-time buyers only, and one program which offers subsidies to low-income borrowers.

In addition to standard home loans, FHA financing covers a wide range of applications, from mobile homes and condominiums to investment property and home improvement loans. Before choosing conventional financing, find out what FHA has to offer. In many cases, an FHA loan will be cheaper to obtain and easier to qualify for.

Where To Apply For A FHA Loan
Since HUD/FHA is an insurer rather than a lender, you must apply for a loan at a lending institution that handles FHA financing. You should have no difficulty finding a lender, since at least half of Oregon's conventional lending institutions (banks, S&Ls and mortgage brokers) also offer FHA real estate loans.

Some institutions are what is known as Direct Endorsement Lenders. They have the in-house ability to process FHA loans, doing the appraisal and credit underwriting themselves, then applying to HUD/FHA for the insurance. This can save the borrower time, since documents do not have to be mailed to and from HUD for processing. Some Direct Endorsement Lenders, however, do not handle all of their loans internally. Questionable applications will often be sent to FHA for processing.

Applying to a Direct Endorsement Lender is no guarantee for quick service on an FHA loan. Of more importance is the efficiency of the loan officer and staff of the lending institution in preparing the necessary paperwork. I have had equally speedy results from both types of lenders and would choose an institution on the basis of past performance, rather than whether or not it is a Direct Endorsement Lender.

Interest Rates On FHA Loans
Until November 1983, HUD established maximum interest rates for all FHA loans. At that time a law was signed, giving lenders and borrowers the right to determine a rate that is agreeable to them. (The one exception to this is the 235 subsidized program, where the interest rate is still set by HUD.)

There is no longer one nationwide rate for a particular type of loan. If you ask three different lenders what rate they charge, you will get three different answers. In fact, you will probably hear three different rates from each institution. For example, one lender might offer FHA loans at 12.5%, 12% and 11.5%. Another will give a different range of numbers. Shop carefully. There are bargains available but there are also hidden costs behind the interest figures. The 12.5% loan, for instance, will be accompanied by a smaller number of discount points than the 12% loan, and the 11.5% loan will have the largest number of points.

Discount Points
Discount points are a form of prepaid interest, charged by the lender at closing. One discount point equals one percent of the loan amount. As an example, on a $50,000 loan, one point would cost $500, one-half of one point would be $250 and two points would be $1,000.

While discount points used to be a feature of FHA and VA financing only, they are being used today with many conventional loans, too. In any kind of financing, the payment of discount points actually results in a buydown of the interest rate. Since the deregulation, it is now possible to obtain an FHA loan without points by paying a higher interest rate.

Before the legislative change, FHA buyers were prohibited from paying the cost of the points. That was the responsibility of the sellers. Since 1983, however, either party may pay the points, except on the Section 235 loans, where points must still be paid by the seller.

In the past, the mention of discount points drove many sellers into a frenzy. This was perfectly understandable. On closing day, the official FHA points could be up to 10 or 12 and the poor seller would have no choice but to pay them or postpone the sale. Now points are not the frightening monster they were. Today the lender, buyer and seller can work together to find a combination of interest rate and points that keeps everyone happy.

Locking The Rate And Points
Some lenders will agree to lock the interest rate and discount points from the date of loan application, for a certain length of time (usually 30, 60 or 90 days). If the rate or points increase, the original figures will be honored if the closing takes place within that time. Borrowers who choose the lock usually pay a slightly higher interest rate, perhaps ½ of 1%, or the lender may charge extra points for this service. Be sure to ask your loan officer what the lender's policy will be if the rates and points drop during the lock period. Some institutions will rewrite the loan at the lower figures; others stick to their original agreement.

Tax And Insurance Reserves
A reserve account for property taxes and homeowner's insurance is required on all FHA loans. In other words, the lender must pay the taxes and insurance directly, out of a fund established by the borrower at closing. The monthly payment on every FHA loan includes not only principal and interest, but also one month's worth of taxes and insurance. Reserve accounts are commonly found in conventional financing too, especially on loans over 80% LTV. With a lower LTV ratio on a conventional loan, the borrower has a choice of whether or not to have a reserve account. In FHA, the reserves are mandatory.

A Misconception About FHA

I have encountered dozens of homeowners who refuse at first to consider an FHA sale because they are convinced that they will be required to repaint the home from top to bottom, even if it is already in good condition. Or they are certain FHA will require a brand new roof, when a conventional lender will say the present one is just fine.

FHA does require its appraisers to check the attic for R-19 insulation and go into the crawl space to look for a plastic sheeting vapor barrier, while many conventional lenders do not specify this. But today, in general, the two are similar in their standards.

Assumability Of An FHA Loan

Unlike most conventional loans available these days, FHA loans may be easily assumed, with an attractively low assumption fee. This is an important benefit for borrowers who know they will be selling the home before the loan is repaid.

There are two ways an FHA loan may be assumed, depending upon the wishes of the seller and buyer. For a $45 assumption fee, HUD permits a "simple" (or "blind") assumption of the loan. The new buyer does not need to qualify for the monthly payments and the seller remains in a position of liability. If the seller wishes a release of liability, a formal application is necessary and HUD must approve the buyer's qualification. This type of assumption carries a fee of $150. (HUD is considering changes in assumption policy, so check with a loan officer for the latest details.)

Section 235 loans, which will be discussed later, are also assumable, even though they have subsidized payments. The sudsidy, however, will end and the payments will return to the unsubsidized level unless the new buyer qualifies for the subsidy.

Types Of FHA Loans

The types, sub-types and intricate details of FHA financing could fill several volumes. Borrowers, sellers and real estate agents need to know only the basics: what loans are available and what are the general guidelines for obtaining these loans. The stickier points of financing are best left to loan officers and HUD itself.

Here is a chart showing the HUD/FHA loan programs available in Oregon. Some, such as the 203b and the 245a are offered by most FHA lenders. Yet for some of the little-used programs, it may be difficult to find a lender willing to handle them.

After the chart, each loan program will be explained in detail. Since the FHA loans are similar to the conventional loans discussed earlier in this book, turn back to that section for information about the basic loan types, such as fixed-rate, adjustable-rate, graduated-payment and GEM loans. As you study this chapter, please remember that loan limits and policies are subject to change by HUD/FHA.

FHA LOANS AT A GLANCE	203b	203 FHA/VA	245a	245b	245 GEM	251 ARM	234c	203k	221d2	235
Single-family home	★	★	★	★	★	★	★	★	★	★
Duplex to four-plex	★	★					★	★		
Owner-occupied	★	★	★	★	★	★	★	★	★	★
Non-Owner-Occupied	★						1	★		
Refinances	★						★	★		
First-time buyers only			★							★
Existing construction	★	★	★			★	★	★	★	★
New construction	★	★	★	★	★	★	★		★	★
Unregulated interest rate	★	★	★	★	★	★	★	★	★	
Interest rate set by HUD										★
Fixed rate	★	★	★	★	★		★	★	★	★
Adjustable rate						2				
Level payments	★	★					★	★	★	3
Negative amortization			★	★						
One-time MIP	★	★	★	★	★	1				
Monthly MIP							★	★	★	★
Buyer may pay points	★	★	★	★	★	★	★	★	★	

1. Varies.
2. ARMs may be used in conjunction with other FHA loan programs.
3. Varies with income but base payments are level.

SECTION 203b: THE BASIC FHA LOAN

This loan, known as the 203b, is the most common of the FHA programs. It is a standard fixed-rate loan with a maximum term of 30 years. 15-year terms are also offered by many lenders. The 203b may be used to buy or refinance one- to four-family homes and mobile homes on owned (not rented) lots, by either occupant or non-occupant borrowers.

Maximum Loan Limits

Most FHA loan programs have two maximum loan amounts: one for the Portland Metropolitan Statistical Area (Multnomah, Clackamas and Washington counties in Oregon, Clark County in Washington), the second for the remained of Oregon. These limits reflect the difference in property values in the two areas and are increased from time to time.

Occupant borrower:	Portland MSA	Other Oregon
single family	$ 86,450	$ 85,200
duplex	$ 97,350	$ 95,950
triplex	$118,300	$116,600
4-flex	$136,500	$134,550

Non-occupant borrower: Maximum loan will be whichever is less: the limit shown above or 85% of the value or purchase price, plus closing costs.

Maximum Loan When Refinancing

Occupant borrower:
1. If you wish to replace an existing loan, the 203b will cover your previous loan amount plus cost of repairs, closing and discount points.
2. To refinance for cash proceeds not related to the property, you may borrow up to 85% of the FHA appraised value plus closing costs.

Non-occupant borrower: Maximum loan will be which ever is less: the limit shown above or 85% of the value plus closing costs. No cash proceeds are allowed.

Loan-To-Value Ratio
Owner-occupied:
1.   97% of the first $25,000 of total FHA value including closing costs and 95% of the remainder over $25,000.
2.   For the purchase of homes $50,000 or less: 97% of the FHA value.
3.   For new construction, up to 1 year old: 90% of total FHA value including closing costs.
4.   For mobile homes on owned lots: 90% of the total FHA value plus closing costs if the home was not HUD approved before construction or has not been permanently placed on its site for more than a year. If approved, or over a year, the standard LTV in 1. and 2. above will apply.

Non-owner occupied: May not exceed 85% LTV.

Calculating The Maximum 203b Loan
When calculating how large a 203b loan you may borrow, take the appraised FHA value of the property and add the FHA Allowable Closing Costs as shown in the chart in Appendix . (These are not the actual closing costs you will be charged; they are used only for the purpose of determining the maximum loan amount.)

Use the sum of the value plus closing costs and the loan-to-value ratio that applies to your situation to calculate the maximum possible 203b loan. Here is an example, using a 3-year old home appraised at $50,000:

Value plus closing costs:
$50,000 + $950 = $50,950

97% of the first $25,000 = $24,250

95% of the remainder ($25,950) = $24,652.50

$48,902.50

Since FHA loans are always rounded down to the nearest $50, the maximum 203b loan for this property would be $48,900.

Mortgage Insurance
The mortgage insurance premium (MIP) on 203b loans is known as a One-Time MIP, although it may be paid in two ways:
1.   It may be paid in cash at closing. For a 30-year loan the MIP would equal .03661 times the mortgage

amount. On a $50,000 loan, for example the MIP would be:

$50,000 X .03661 = $1,830.50

If the entire MIP is paid in cash at closing, there will be no additional monthly premiums.

2. Or the entire MIP may be financed. In this case, the total amount of the MIP will be added to the loan amount and this figure will be used to calculate the monthly payment.

From our example above:

100% of the MIP	= $ 1,830.50
Loan Amount	= $50,000.00
Total	= $51,830.50

This total amount may be financed. Note, however, that these are the only two alternatives. It is not possible, for instance, to pay 50% of the MIP in cash, while financing the balance.

If the loan is repaid in full within the first ten years (of a 30-year loan), HUD will refund the unearned portion of the MIP to the mortgagor (borrower). This does not apply to assumptions since the loan remains in effect. Sellers who paid the MIP in cash at closing may, if they wish, ask the buyers who are assuming the loan to reimburse them for part of the MIP. If the MIP was financed, the new buyers can assume it, with no change in the payment or terms.

SECTION 203: VETERAN LOAN

This loan, also known as the FHA/VA loan, is similar to the 203b but is restricted to qualified veterans who wish to finance owner-occupied, single-family property only. Mobile homes permanently placed on individual (owned) lots are also included. Veterans may have any number of FHA/VA loans that they qualify for but all must be for owner-occupied homes.

The maximum loan amount, term of the loan and mortgage insurance are identical to those of the 203b. Refer to that section for the details. What does vary is the loan-to-value ratio, a more generous ratio for veterans.

Loan-To-Value Ratio

1. The standard loan-to-value ratio for FHA/VA loans is 100% of the first $25,000 of FHA's appraised value including closing costs, then 95% of the remainder above $25,000.
2. For new construction less than one year old, the maximum LTV is 90% of the FHA value plus closing costs.
3. Mobile homes on owned lots will qualify for the high LTV ratio only if they have been permanently situated for more than one year or are proposed construction to be built to HUD guidelines. All others will have a maximum LTV of 90%.

Veteran Eligibility

To be eligible for a FHA/VA loan, a veteran must have served at least ninety days of active duty and must obtain a Veteran's Certificate of Status from the Veterans Administration.

SECTION 245a:
THE GRADUATED-PAYMENT LOAN

The 245a is a popular FHA loan program when interest rates are high. (When rates are low, most borrowers prefer the 203b.) This fixed-rate, graduated-payment loan may be used only for the purchase of an owner-occupied single-family home (including mobile homes on owned lots).

If you have read the chapter dealing with graduated payment loans (in the Conventional Loans section of this book), you will remember that a true graduated payment loan has a fixed rate of interest plus monthly payments that start at a lower level than those of a standard amortized loan. The payments are increased at specific intervals (in this case, yearly) until they reach a level which will pay off the loan in a total of thirty years.

Deferred Interest

With any graduated payment loan, negative amortization (also known as "deferred interest") is an unavoidable feature. Because the initial payments are not large enough to cover the amount of interest due, let alone any left over to reduce the principal, the unpaid interest is deferred by adding it to the loan balance. In the early years of the loan, the loan balance actually

84

increases. The amount of the increase depends upon the level of the original starting payment and the size of the yearly payment jumps.

Variety Of 245a Plans Available
There are five different 245a loan plans, but most lenders offer only Plan III. Some also handle Plans I and II. At the present time, I do not know of a lending institution offering Plans IV and V, but I will include them here for your information.

The five plans differ in several respects:
* loan-to-value ratio
* required down payment
* level of initial payment
* percentage of payment increase yearly
* number of yearly increases

In general, the rule is as follows: the higher the initial payment and the shorter the catching-up period, the smaller the amount of deferred interest and the smaller the required down payment. In all cases, 245a loans require larger down payments than 203b loans. The additional down payment on a 245a loan can range from less than 1% to over 6% of the value of the home, depending upon which plan is chosen.

Calculating The Maximum 245a Loan
The maximum loan possible with any 245a loan is $86,450 for the Portland metropolitan area and $85,200 for the rest of Oregon. But the various plans each use a different factor to determine the loan-to-value ratio; that is, how much down payment will be required for a particular size of loan. Here is how to calculate it:

1. Appraised Value plus FHA Allowable Closing Costs (see Allowable Closing Costs chart in Appendix)
2. Multiply this total by .97
3. Divide your answer by the factor for the plan you have chosen, from the following chart.

Plan Number	Yearly Payment Increase	Number Of Years of Increases	Maximum Loan Factor
I	2½%	5	1.0194929
II	5%	5	1.0530311
III	7½%	5	1.0871331
IV	2%	10	1.0465419
V	3%	10	1.0877544

Let's take, as an example, a home appraised at $50,000. According to the chart in the Appendix, the Allowable Closing Costs would be $950. Add the two and then multiply by .97: $50,950 X .97 = $49,421.50
Now divide by one of the factors (we'll choose Plan I):
    49,421.50 ÷ 1.0194929 = $48,476.55
Because FHA loans are always rounded down to the nearest $50, the maximum loan amount for a $50,000 home under Plan I will be $48,450. (A 203b loan for the same home could go as high as $48,900.)

Note: For the purchase of homes $50,000 or less, the loan-to-value ratio can be as high as 97%.

The Starting Payments
The various 245a plans each have different starting payment levels. Since loan officers use the amount of the initial payment to qualify a borrower, those plans with the lowest starting levels will require less income to qualify for.

Starting payments are determined with the use of a chart, based on the interest rate of the loan. As an example, here is a chart for a 12.75% loan. One column shows the first year's monthly payment for each $1,000 of loan amount. (For a $60,000 loan, for instance, multiply the payment by 60.) The next column shows what the starting payment would be on our $50,000 home with the maximum loan. Compare each of these to the monthly payment on a maximum 203b loan for the same property, at the same interest rate: $531.54.

Plan Number	Based on 12.75% Starting Payment Rate	$50,000 Property	
		Maximum Loan Amount	Starting Payment
I	$9.97 per $1000	$48,450	$483.05
II	$9.15 per $1000	$46,900	$429.14
III	$8.40 per $1000	$45,450	$381.78
IV	$9.78 per $1000	$47,200	$461.62
V	$9.26 per $1000	$45,400	$420.40

Remember that the interest rate remains the same throughout the life of the loan but the payments increase according to the specific plan chosen. For our example above in Plan III, which has five yearly increases of 7½%, the monthly payment for the second year would be 1.075 times the starting payment (1.075 X 381.78 = $410.41). To calculate the third year's payment, multiply the second year's payment, $410.41, by 1.075.

Mortgage Insurance On A 245a Loan

The mortgage insurance premium on a 245a loan is a One-Time MIP similar to that on the 203b. Follow the 203b directions to determine the cost.

SECTION 245b:
NEW HOME PURCHASE PROGRAM

This program was designed to enable borrowers who have not owned a home in the three years before loan application to buy a new or substantially rehabilitated home. It is open only to those applicants who are unable to qualify for financing under Section 245a or any other FHA loan program. The number of 245b loans is limited. Each HUD area office is given an allocation for a certain number of units to be financed and when this limit is reached, no additional loans will be available until a new allocation has been made.

Loan Limits And LTV Ratio

Although the maximum loan limit is the same as that of 245a loans, namely $86,450 for the Portland area and $85,200 for the rest of Oregon, the loan-to-value ratio on 245b loans is often higher. That means, in many cases, a lower down payment is possible. The loan-to-value ratio and down payment are calculated on a sliding scale, depending upon the interest rate and the specific loan plan used.

Loan Plans Available

There are two graduated payment loans available under this program. One has increases of 7.5% per year for five years, the other has 4.9% increases yearly for ten years.

SECTION 245 GEM LOANS

The FHA Growing Equity Mortgage program has been rarely used by lenders. It is a standard GEM loan, with no deferred interest. The interest rate is fixed but the monthly payments increase annually by 2% or 3%, depending upon the plan chosen. As a result, the loan is paid in full in a term that is much shorter than the typical 30 years. Maximum loan amounts, loan-to-value ratio and mortgage insurance are similar to the 203b loans, but unlike 203b, the GEM loans are not available for refinancing a home. New or older homes, as well as mobile homes on owned property, may be financed.

SECTION 251:
ADJUSTABLE RATE MORTGAGE LOANS

HUD introduced the FHA ARM loan, with plenty of hoopla, in August 1984. Its reception by the lenders was frosty. Very, very few ARM loans have been written since then and most lenders are not willing to handle the program. If you want an adjustable rate loan, there are many excellent conventional programs available today.

In general, the Section 251 program is an adjustable rate loan, using as its index the weekly yield on U.S. Treasury Securities. It has annual rate adjustments, with an annual cap of 1% and a lifetime cap of 5%. Loans are available for owner-occupied property only, new or existing single- to four-family homes, mobile homes and condominiums. Refinances are permitted.

SECTION 234c: CONDOMINIUM LOANS

Section 234c loans are used to finance (or refinance) new or existing condominium units that have been approved by FHA, VA or FNMA. Borrowers who currently have 234c financing for their own residences may purchase up to three units on a non-occupant basis.

Maximum Loan Limits And Loan-To-Value Ratio

For owner-occupied units, the maximum loan is $86,450 in the Portland area and $85,200 for the rest of Oregon. The LTV ratio is similar to that for 203b loans.

Graduated payment plans and adjustable rate loans are also available to condominium borrowers. There, other LTV ratios will apply, as specified for those types of loans.

Mortgage Insurance
The mortgage insurance for Section 234c loans is not collected on a one-time basis but is paid monthly at the rate of ½ of 1% of the loan amount per annum. On a $50,000 loan, this would mean a premium of approximately $20 per month added to the regular monthly payment.

SECTION 203k: REHABILITATION LOANS

The FHA 203k loan allows a borrower to finance the purchase of a "fixer-upper" plus the cost of repairs necessary to bring it up to FHA standards. With other types of financing, any problems must be corrected before closing; with the 203k, the closing may take place before rehabilitation has begun. Funds for the repairs will be held in escrow and released as each phase of the work is completed.

It is difficult to find a lender willing to provide 203k financing. The paperwork is considerable and most institutions would rather not tackle it. I have included the 203k program in this book because you may be lucky enough to find a cooperative lender.

Loan Information
Maximum loan amounts and the loan-to-value ratio are the same as those on a 203b loan. The loan may include the value of the property at the time of purchase plus the cost of the rehabilitiation. This total may not exceed the 203b limits.

Existing one- to four-unit homes are eligible for 203k financing (or refinancing). They may be either owner- or non-owner-occupied.

Mortgage insurance is paid monthly, rather than being paid or financed at closing. The yearly charge is ½ of 1% of the loan amount; divide by 12 for the monthly premium.

SECTION 221d2 LOANS

There are two reasons why this loan program is not often used. First, the loan limits are very low: from $36,000 to $42,000 (the higher amount for a 4-bedroom home and a family of five). Second, a city code inspection must be made, and electrical and plumbing inspections may also be required. If the code inspector finds evidence that the home does not comply with code standards, the owner must make the necessary repairs, even if the loan is not granted. This is not a popular program with sellers!

The only advantage this loan has over the 203b is its loan-to-value ratio. In most cases, up to a 98% loan is possible, except on mobile homes which have been on the site (not a rented lot) for less than one year. Then the LTV is 90%. Mortgage insurance is paid monthly, at the rate of $\frac{1}{2}$ of 1% of the loan amount per annum.

SECTION 235: SUBSIDIZED LOANS

Each year, in October, the area HUD office receives an allocated number of Section 235 loan units. These are loans with payments that are subsidized by the federal government for borrowers who are unable to qualify for the full amount of the payment.

Property Qualifications

The home to be financed must be either a new home built with FHA, VA or FmHA approval (or one with a HOW warranty), or it must have undergone substantial rehabilitation (over 25% of the value of the property). The sales price is limited to $57,000 for a 3-bedroom home and $66,000 for a 4-bedroom with five or more family members.

Maximum Loan And Minimum Down Payment Amounts

A borrower must have at least 3% of the property value as down payment. The maximum loan for a 3-bedroom home is $47,500, with up to $55,000 for a 4-bedroom.

Borrower Qualifications

Borrowers may not be single persons, unless handicapped or over 62 years of age. They must be family units, defined by HUD as "two or more people related by blood, marriage or operation of law". There are maximum income limits which Section 235 borrowers may not exceed. These limits vary with the size of the family and the location of the home. For instance, the current income range for a 4-person family is $21,700 to $27,350 for different parts of the state.

Payment Subsidies
Borrowers must pay a minimum of 28% of their adjusted gross income. If they are unable to pay the entire monthly payment, they may be eligible for a government subsidy, covering a portion of the amount due. With a 12.5% interest rate loan, for example, the borrower's payment could be based on an interest rate as low as 4%. The subsidy may last as long as 10 years, but income recertification is required annually. The amount of the subsidy must be repaid from the property appreciation if the home is resold or rented for more than a year.

Interest Rate On Section 235 Loans
The interest rate on these loans is set by HUD/FHA and, unlike other programs, the buyer is not permitted to pay discount points.

SHARED EQUITY LOANS
"Equity participation" is a popular term in real estate circles today. FHA has a program for shared equity loans involving an occupant/mortgagor and a non-occupant or investor/mortgagor. According to FHA guidelines, the combined incomes of both parties must be sufficient to cover the monthly expenses on the property, but each individual's income must qualify for a certain percentage of the expenses. An occupant/mortgagor must qualify for at least 55% of the total monthly cost; an investor/mortgagor requires at least 25% participation. An exception to this rule may be made when there is a close and obvious connection between the two parties, such as a relationship by blood or marriage, or a business partnership.

HOME IMPROVEMENT LOANS
FHA also insures second- and third-mortgage loans. These are fixed-rate loans of up to 15 years and are available through credit unions, mortgage companies

and other institutional lenders. The current maximum limits are $17,500 for a loan secured by real property and $2,500 for an unsecured loan, such as a loan for a mobile home on a rented lot. The funds must be used for non-luxury improvements that are permanently attached to the home. Sorry, no new drapes.

MOBILE HOME LOANS

A mobile home permanently sited on land that is owned by the borrower is considered real property and is financed by the standard FHA home loans discussed above. But HUD also has loan programs for mobile homes that will be placed on rented lots. These loans, with a maximum loan amount of $40,500 for either single-wide or double-wide homes, are available for new homes only. The standard term is twenty years. Many lending institutions handle these loans as well as the full range of FHA real estate financing.

ADVANTAGES OF FHA FINANCING

1. Higher loan-to-value ratio, as compared to conventional financing.
2. Easily assumed.
3. Lower loan fee than conventional loans.
4. Wide variety of loan programs available, including one subsidized program for low-income borrowers.
5. Choice of interest rate and discount points
6. Points may be paid by either party.

DISADVANTAGES OF FHA FINANCING

1. Maximum loan amounts are lower than conventional limits.
2. Mortgage insurance is required on all loans. MIP is an added expense at closing or monthly.

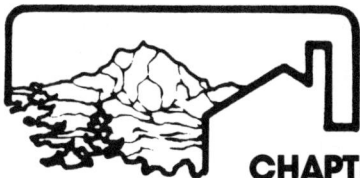

CHAPTER 13

VA Loans

DEFINITION: **The Veterans Administration offers a loan guaranty to lenders who provide attractive lower-interest, no-down-payment loans to qualified veterans.**

If you are a veteran and want to finance a home, pay particular attention to the three loan programs designed especially for you: the FHA/VA and Veterans Administration programs, both established by the federal government, and the Oregon State Department of Veterans' Affairs loans, which will be covered in the following chapter.

Of the three, the Veterans Administration (VA) program is the only one where no down payment is required for many loans. Add to this the benefits of a lower-than-conventional interest rate, minimum closing costs and easier qualifying standards, and you will see why this is an excellent loan to consider.

The VA Loan Guaranty
VA offers only a loan guaranty, not the actual funds, to institutional lenders who provide the loans according to VA standards. Just as the FHA insurance program protects lenders against default, so the VA guaranty covers a lender's loss at time of foreclosure. This is not an insurance program and so there is no mortgage insurance premium to be paid. The only additional fee charged (above the standard fees and closing costs) is a VA funding fee of 1% of the loan amount.

Veteran's Eligibility
The first step in obtaining a loan is to have VA determine your eligibility. If your meet the requirements, VA will issue a Certificate Of Eligibility that will enable you to

apply for a VA loan. (Note that FHA/VA and Oregon DVA loans have different eligibility requirements. While DVA is more restrictive in its standards, FHA will accept many ex-servicemen, such as World War I veterans, who are not eligible for VA loans.)

The number of days of active duty required by VA depends upon the dates of service. Here are the three service categories:

1. Wartime Service: If you served anytime during
   * World War II (September 16, 1940 to July 25, 1947)
   * Korean Conflict (June 27, 1950 to January 31, 1955) or
   * Vietnam Era (August 5, 1964 to May 7, 1975)
   you must have served at least 90 days of active duty and must have received other than a dishonorable discharge. The 90-day limit may be waived if you were discharged because of a service-related disability.

2. Peacetime Service: If your service fell entirely within one of these periods:
   * July 26, 1947 to June 26, 1950
   * February 1, 1955 to August 4, 1964, or
   * May 8, 1975 to September 7, 1980 (if enlisted) or to   October 16, 1981 (if officer)
   you must have served at least 181 days of continuous active duty and received other than a dishonorable discharge. Again, that 181-day requirement may be shortened if you were discharged because of a service-related disability.

3. Recent Service: If you were separated from service which began after these dates:
   * September 7, 1980 (enlisted personnel) or
   * October 16, 1981 (officers)
   you must have completed 24 months of continuous active duty or the full period (at least 181 days) for which you were called or ordered to active duty, and you must have received other than a dishonorable discharge; or you must have completed at least 181 days of active duty with a hardship discharge, a discharge for the convenience of the government.   94

Alternatively, you must have been determined to have a compensable service-connected disability or have been discharged for such a disability.

Other persons are eligible to receive a VA loan:

4. Service personnel currently on active duty, who have served at least 181 days on continuous active status, regardless of when the service began.

5. Unmarried surviving spouses of eligible persons who died as the result of service-connected injuries.

6. The spouse of an active-duty member of the Armed Forces listed for over 90 days as missing in action or a prisoner of war.

7. Certain U.S. citizens who served in the armed forces of a government allied with the United States in World War II.

8. Individuals with service as members in certain other organizations, services, programs and schools may be eligible. VA will determine if such service may qualify.

To obtain a certificate of eligibility, request Form 26-1880 from the nearest VA office. The regional office for Oregon is:

VA Regional Office
Federal Building
1220 SW 3rd Avenue
Portland, OR 97204

If you cannot find your original discharge papers to accompany the completed form, ask a benefits counselor at the VA office to help you obtain a Certificate in Lieu of Lost or Destroyed Discharge.

Where To Apply For A VA Loan
Since the Veterans Administration is not a lender, you must apply for a loan at a lending institution that handles VA loans. This should be easy to do, since many conventional lenders (banks, S&Ls, mortgage companies and mortgage brokers) also offer both FHA

and VA loan programs. The Veterans Administration regional office noted above will provide a list of names of local lenders, if you are unable to find one near you.

Lenders process VA loans in one of two ways. Some institutions have the authority to handle the loans on an "automatic" basis. These lenders are able to make the necessary credit decision and may proceed with the loan closing without waiting for VA approval. Other institutions handle VA loans on a "prior approval" basis; they must send all the pertinent information to VA to be evaluated. If the loan package is approved, the lender receives a certificate of guaranty and the closing may then take place. Both types of lenders must order an appraisal from VA; the only difference is in the approval of the credit information. Automatic processing can save time, but the efficiency of a lender is still the biggest factor in getting a loan closed quickly.

Entitlement: How Large A Loan?
VA does not limit the size of loan a veteran may receive. It does, however, limit the size of the loan guaranty. In case of foreclosure, the lender will be reimbursed only up to the amount of the guaranty. This, indirectly, limits the size of loan, since lenders are cautious about stepping out on a limb. VA loans with no down payment (that is, 100% LTV) are commonly offered in an amount four times the guaranty. With additional money as down payment, a borrower can receive a larger loan, according to the particular lender's policy.

The size of the guaranty is known as the veteran's "entitlement", a standard amount which is established by the Veterans Administration. The original entitlement level was $2,000 but that amount has been increased several times and is now $27,500. Using the guidelines above, we can determine that the maximum 100% LTV loan offered by most lenders will be four times $27,500, or $110,000.

Each eligible veteran is allowed the full amount of the entitlement. When veterans receive a VA home loan, they "use" that entitlement. They may not receive another VA loan until one of two situations occurs.

If the property is sold and the loan is paid in full or transferred to another eligible veteran who agrees to use his or her entitlement, then the original borrower's entitlement can be restored and used for another loan.

If the Veterans Administration increases the entitlement, a veteran may receive new financing based upon the difference between the entitlement used previously and the new entitlement level. For example, a veteran purchasing a home in 1974 would have had a $12,500 entitlement. Even if a non-veteran had assumed the loan and had not as yet repaid it, the veteran would still have a $15,000 entitlement today ($27,500 − $12,500). Most lenders would offer the veteran a new loan up to $60,000 with no down payment.

In no case may the loan amount exceed the value of the property or the purchase price, whichever is less. The value, as determined by the Veterans Administration, is the figure shown on the Certificate of Reasonable Value (CRV), the VA appraisal required with each loan application.

Interest Rate And Discount Points On VA Loans
The interest rate for all VA loans is set by the Veterans Administration. Because the VA's goal is to help eligible veterans buy homes, the rate is somewhat lower than rates on conventional loans. But why would a lender voluntarily loan money at an interest rate below that earned on other loans? The answer is this: through the use of discount points, the lender is recompensed for accepting less interest. (To understand the use of points, read the previous chapter on FHA loans.) Discount points are a form of interest, paid to the lender at closing. When there is a wide spread between the current VA and conventional rates, the number of discount points paid will be high. If the VA rate is close to the conventional rates, then fewer points will be charged.

Unlike most FHA transactions, where either party may pay the discount points, VA requires the seller to pay them, except in certain cases. One example is for a refinance or home improvement loan. There the borrower may, and in fact, must pay the points.

Tax And Insurance Reserves

As with FHA financing, the monthly payment on a VA loan includes an additional amount to cover 1/12th of both the annual property tax and homeowner's insurance premium. Payment to the county tax office and the insurance company will be made annually by the lender.

Assumability Of A VA Loan

VA loans may be assumed in one of two ways. New buyers who are eligible veterans may use their entitlement to assume a loan. They must qualify for the assumption as though it were a new loan, presenting a satisfactory credit report and clear financial picture. In this case, the seller will be released from liability and the new buyer will step into the seller's shoes, assuming the loan at the original interest rate and terms.

The second type of assumption on VA loans is the simple, or blind, assumption. Here it is not necessary for the buyer to be a veteran or to qualify for the loan, but the seller retains some liability in case of default. (Read the chapter on Assumptions for more information.) It is possible for a person with a badly scarred credit rating to assume a VA loan in this manner. VA doesn't care, but the seller (who will not be released from liability) might object. In a simple assumption also, the interest rate and terms remain the same, making these very attractive loans to assume.

Types Of Loans Available

VA loans may be used to finance or refinance a home, new or old. Mobile home and condominium loans are also available. The veteran borrower must occupy the home within a reasonable amount of time after closing; non-owner-occupied property may not be financed. Loans for multi-unit buildings are available (up to a 4-plex for one veteran), but the veteran must occupy one of the units. Borrowers who depend upon rental income from the building to qualify for the loan, must show proof that they have the background or skills to be a successful landlord, plus sufficient cash reserves to make 6 months of loan payments without the rental income.

VA guarantees three different loan plans: the traditional fixed-rate loan, the graduated payment mortgage (GPM)

98

loan, and the growing equity mortgage (GEM) loan. Temporary buydowns up to five years of duration are also available. These loans and buydowns are similar in structure to their conventional counterparts. Study the Conventional Loans section for the basic information about each method. Here, however, are the specific VA details.

VA TRADITIONAL FIXED-RATE MORTGAGE LOANS

The fixed-rate mortgage loans guaranteed by the Veterans Administration are standard loans with a maximum term of 30 years and 32 days. Recently, 15-year loans have gained in popularity and are offered by many lenders.

VA gives the lenders certain latitude in lending practice, provided minimum standards are met. For example, on a fixed-rate loan, VA does not require a down payment if the purchase price or cost does not exceed the reasonable value of the property, yet a lender may ask for one. The lending institution around the corner may have a slightly different requirement.

The traditional fixed-rate mortgage loan is widely available. Less often used are the other two loans, the GEMs and the GPMs.

VA GROWING EQUITY MORTGAGE LOANS

VA guarantees GEM loans and is willing to consider various plans the lenders may offer. An acceptable GEM must have payment increases that are moderate and easy to handle, for example, 3% per year for ten years. Borrowers will find a wide variety of GEM plans designed by the lending institutions and approved by the Veterans Administration. They are typically based on 30-year terms, but the increasing payments lead to an early payoff, in roughly half the time. The initial payment level is also based on the straight-payment 30-year loan. VA GEMs may not have payments that are insufficient to cover the interest due; in other words, deferred interest is not permitted.

VA will also guarantee GEMs whose payment increases are tied to an index, rather than a fixed, predetermined increase amount but few lenders offer this type of GEM.

VA GRADUATED PAYMENT MORTGAGE LOANS

There is one GPM plan approved for a VA guaranty. It is similar to HUD/FHA's Section 245 Plan III loan, discussed in the last chapter. This plan has annual loan payment increases of 7.5% for the first five years. From the sixth year, the payments remain level for the remaining term. Like the GEM, it is a fixed-rate loan and is based on a 30-year amortization. Unlike the GEM, the initial monthly payments are too low to cover the entire amount of interest due. This, of course, means deferred interest (negative amortization) and an increasing loan balance for the first few years of the loan.

Because of this, VA has set different down payment requirements for the GPM. Lenders must ask for a cash down payment equal to the highest amount of negative amortization that will occur. Borrowers may, if they wish, make a larger down payment, but the maximum loan amount is limited to the appraised value (CRV) less the highest amount of negative amortization.

The low starting payment will be used as a basis for qualifying borrowers. As a result, GPMs are easier to qualify for; the income needed is considerably lower than that for the other two types of VA loans.

GPMs may not be used to refinance a home that is presently owned but a GPM may be replaced by a level-payment VA loan at a lower rate of interest.

MOBILE HOME LOANS

Mobile homes on borrower-owned land are financed by the VA mortgage loans discussed above. VA will guarantee loans for new or used mobile homes on rented lots, but at the present time, it is difficult to find a lender who will finance a used home. A mobile home dealer can direct you to a VA lender who handles this type of loan.

HOME IMPROVEMENT LOANS

VA home improvement loans are rarely written, although VA will guarantee second mortgage loans to qualified veterans. Few, if any, lenders here offer this program, preferring instead to use FHA or conventional plans.

AUTOMATIC PROCESSING PROGRAM

Some lenders now have the authority to process VA loans, without sending the documents to the Veterans Administration for approval before closing. (The CRV must still be done by a VA appraiser, though.) This can reduce the processing time considerably, so if a quick closing is important, find a lender who offers the program.

ADVANTAGES OF VA LOANS

1. Up to 100% LTV ratio possible.
2. Attractive interest rate.
3. Easier to qualify for than conventional financing.
4. Easy to assume.
5. No mortgage insurance premium to pay.

DISADVANTAGES OF VA LOANS

1. Discount points are charged.
2. Points must be paid by the seller; buyer may not assist.

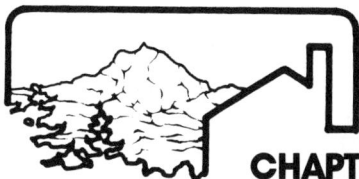

CHAPTER 14
Oregon DVA Loans

DEFINITION: The Oregon Department of Veterans' Affairs offers variable-rate loans at below-market rates to qualified Oregon veterans (and eligible spouses) for the purpose of acquiring a house or farm as a primary home.

Oregon veterans are fortunate to have three excellent loan programs to choose from: FHA/VA and Federal VA loans discussed in previous chapters, and Oregon DVA, also known as State GI loans. They are run by two entirely different levels of government, have different lending requirements, and offer very different types of financing. If you have received a loan from any one of the three, you may still obtain financing from the others, provided that you meet the eligibility standards.

How DVA Loans Are Funded
The DVA loan program is funded entirely through the sale of State of Oregon general obligation bonds. It is not financed through tax dollars. The Department of Veterans' Affairs manages the lending process, from application, through appraisal and approval, to administration of the loans.

Who Is Eligible For A DVA Loan?
The eligibility requirements for Federal VA loans are different from those set by the Oregon DVA. In general, the state standards are considerably stricter. There are two lending categories and an applicant must meet all of the requirements in either category to receive a DVA loan.

Category I: Veterans
a. Must have served honorably at least 210 consecutive days of active duty, with at least a part of that service occurring between September 15, 1940 and December 31, 1976. (The 210-day requirement may be waived if a service-related disability caused an early release.)
b. Must have received a honorable discharge or have been honorably separated to a reserve.
c. Must have been an Oregon resident at the time of entry into active duty or for a total of at least five years since your discharge.
d. Must be an Oregon resident at the time of loan application.

Category II: Spouse of an armed forces member listed as missing in action or a prisoner of war, or surviving spouse of an armed forces member who died on active duty. (There are no requirements for minimum length of service or honorable discharge.)
a. Must be an Oregon resident at time of application (but there is no required length of residency).
b. Must not have remarried.

Eligibility to apply for a loan ends 30 years after a veteran's date of discharge from active duty, or 30 years from the date an eligible spouse was notified of the veteran's death, capture or disappearance. As proof of service, veterans must submit their Report of Separation From Active Duty, Form DD214.

Applicants for a DVA loan must meet credit standards set by the department and have sufficient family income to qualify for the loan. (In a later chapter, "Qualifying For A Loan", the calculations and requirements will be explained.)

Types And Terms Of Loans
DVA offers loans for the purchase or construction of the applicant's primary home (not a vacation home or secondary residence). Farms, houseboats, and mobile homes on owned or rented land may also be financed. In addition, DVA provides loans for non-luxury improvements (energy conservation devices, for example) to DVA-financed property only. Refinances are not permitted.

An eligible applicant many currently borrow up to $63,000 for a home or $185,000 for a farm. This limit is subject to change. Home improvement loans are available only to those borrowers who have not used their maximum loan limit.

DVA may make loans up to 95% of the appraised value of houses and mobile homes with land. For farms, the limit is 90% of the appraised value. The limit for a houseboat or mobile home without land is 85%.

Home and farm loans have maximum terms of 30 years; a mobile home may be financed up to 20 years, depending upon its physical condition.

Variable Interest Rate
All of the loans have a variable interest rate, one that may be increased by DVA during the term of the loan. Previous DVA loans had a 1% interest rate limit set by the state legislature but recent loans do not. Even so, the rates on existing loans have been changed only twice in the program's first forty years.

Rates For New Loans
The interest rate on new loans is established each time bonds are sold. By law it is set at one-half of one percent above the rate offered on the bonds. Traditionally the interest rates on DVA loans are below conventional loan rates, making them very attractive to borrowers. If interest rates, in general, are very high at the time of a proposed bond sale, the sale will be postponed until the bonds can be sold at rates that will allow reasonably priced loans.

One Or Two Loans To A Customer
By state law, an eligible borrower may receive no more than two "counting" loans. (A "counting" loan is one to buy or replace a home; improvement loans or loans made before the law went into effect on October 4, 1977 are "non-counting" loans.) But you must also take into consideration the lending limits ($63,000 for a home, $185,000 for a farm). DVA also requires that the first loan be paid in full or transferred before the second loan is issued.

In other words, if a borrower received a $30,000 loan in 1980, he or she could apply for another home loan for an amount up to $33,000, provided that the $30,000 loan had been repaid or transferred to another person. Or let's look at another example. If the original loan, in the amount of $20,000 for instance, was made before October 4, 1977 and if a second loan (let's say, $23,000) did not use up the allotted $63,000 maximum, the borrower would be eligible for a third loan, up to the current limit. In this case, the borrower has received $43,000 had has had only one "counting" loan. Therefore he or she could borrow an additional $20,000.

Exceptions To The Rule
There are two exceptions to the two-loan rule. The first is called "Restoration of Loan Right". The right to receive another full loan may be granted if any of the following situations occur: loss of the property by fire, flood or condemnation; sale due to job transfer or employment change; and loss of property to the veteran's ex-spouse through divorce. The previous loan must be paid in full or transferred to another person before the new loan is closed. Restoration is not an automatic occurrence; DVA looks at the individual case before deciding whether or not to grant it.

The second exception to the rule applies to veterans who are at least 50% disabled, as certified by the armed forces or the Veterans' Administration. These disabled veterans may have their loan rights restored if medical reasons force them to find another home, if their employer transfers them, or if their spouse is transferred to a job in a different location (provided that the spouse earns over 50% of the household income).

Weatherization Requirements
Homes financed by DVA and built before July 1, 1977, must be brought up to state standards of weatherization. (Homes built since that time have been constructed according to those standards.) A list of required changes will be sent to the borrower after the home has been appraised.

Often the seller will agree to pay for the necessary weatherization but if this is not the case, the cost may sometimes be added to the amount of the loan. However, the total loan, including weatherization costs, may not exceed the maximum loan amount or loan-to-value ratio.

Weatherization requirements may be waived for properties with historic significance, with certification by the State Historic Preservation Office or listing in the National Register of Historic Places.

Building A Home
DVA loans are available for constructing a home and, at the same time, for financing the land on which the home is built. There are specific requirements for new construction that differ from construction loans offered by conventional lenders. If you are planning to build, talk to a DVA loan officer for full details.

To determine the value of the home to be constructed, DVA will appraise the land and study the plans and specifications. Plans must be prepared according to DVA standards and must be submitted to the department before receiving city or county approval. A loan officer will provide necessary cost estimate and value appraisal forms.

DVA does not disburse funds until construction has been completed, except in a situation where the contractor is registered with the Oregon Builders' Board and obtains a performance bond in the full amount of the construction contract. Then partial payments may be made during construction.

A borrower can be reimbursed for money spent on building costs but only if these were paid after loan application or within 10 months before that date. The department will not pay for any work done by a borrower or spouse.

Farm Loans And Mobile Home Financing
In addition to the information included in this chapter, there are some specific requirements for DVA farm and mobile home loans. If you are interested in one of these, contact the nearest DVA office for full details.

Assumability Of A DVA Loan

DVA loans have two different sets of assumption rules, depending upon whether the loan is to be assumed by an eligible veteran or by a person not eligible for a DVA loan.

Eligible borrowers may use their DVA loan right to assume a DVA loan at its existing interest rate. They must apply for the assumption at a DVA office and follow the same procedure as that for a new loan. If the property does not meet the weatherization standards, DVA must insist that it be weatherized before the assumption may take place. (It is possible to finance the weatherization if the borrower has not reached the borrowing limit and can qualify for the additional funds.)

Borrowers who are ineligible for a DVA loan may assume one, however the interest rate on the loan will be increased to the current assumption rate set by DVA each December, with certain exceptions (see below). At the present time, it is not necessary for the buyer to qualify for this type of assumption or even to make application at a DVA office. The paperwork will be ordered and processed by the escrow officer handling the closing.

One exception to the interest increase rule mentioned above concerns loans that were originally assumed before February 3, 1982. These loans may be assumed one more time by an ineligible borrower at the existing interest rate. Also, if the borrower dies or is divorced, the loan may be transferred to the unremarried ex-spouse, surviving spouse, child or stepchild at the existing rate.

There is no limit to the number of times a DVA loan may be transferred to eligible borrowers using their DVA loan rights. However there is a restriction on assumptions to ineligible borrowers. After July 20, 1983, only one such assumption may take place. At the following sale, the loan must be paid in full.

At the time this edition was printed, a moratorium on this rule was in effect. In other words, more than one such assumption may be allowed. Check with DVA for current policy.

Where To Apply For A DVA Loan

Contact the nearest DVA loan servicing office to apply for a loan. A loan officer will be assigned to you and will handle the entire loan application process. If there is no nearby branch office, find out if your county employs a veteran's service officer, who may be able to give you loan information. Here are the loan servicing offices throughout the state:

BEND
155 N. E. Revere Ave.
Bend, OR 97701
        Phone: 388-6122

COOS BAY
455 South Fourth St.
Coos Bay, OR 97420
        Phone: 269-1114

EUGENE-SPRINGFIELD
2073 Olympic Street
Suite 200
Springfield, OR 97477
        Phone: 726-3501

KLAMATH FALLS
Executive Plaza Building
Suite 102
3949 South 6th St.
Klamath Falls, OR 97603
        Phone: 883-5666

MEDFORD
1175 East Main St.
Suite 2B
Medford, OR 97504-7457
        Phone: 776-6050

PENDLETON
700 SE Emigrant
Suite 350
Pendleton, OR 97801
        Phone: 276-8009

PORTLAND AREA

EAST PORTLAND
7931 NE Halsey St.
Suite 302
Portland, OR 97213
        Phone: 257-4320

WEST PORTLAND
Plaza West
9600 SW Oak St.
Suite 340
Portland, OR 97223
        Phone: 293-4100

SALEM
700 Summer St. NE
Suite 100
Salem, OR 97310-1239
        Phone: 373-2067

ADVANTAGES OF DVA LOANS

1. Excellent interest rate.
2. Low loan fees.
3. Easy to qualify.
4. Assumable by veteran or non-veteran.

DISADVANTAGES OF DVA LOANS

1. Low maximum loan amount.
2. Variable interest rate.

CHAPTER 15

Oregon Housing Division Programs

DEFINITION: **The Housing Division of the Oregon Department of Commerce provides funds for the purchase of moderate-priced homes, plus a tax credit program for qualified buyers.**

The Single Family Mortgage Purchase Program was designed to help Oregonians buy a home. It is the lively offspring of the old "Loans-To-Lenders" program, which had a name that was far easier to remember and pronounce. While there is no catchy nickname for the current program, it is well worth keeping in mind during the search for financing.

How The Program Works
The Oregon legislature gives the Housing Division of the Department of Commerce the power to sell revenue bonds. The proceeds from the bond sales are used to finance the Mortgage Purchase Program.

Unlike the Oregon Department of Veteran's Affairs, which manages all aspects of its loan program, the Housing Division turns over much of the responsibility for the Mortgage Purchase Program to institutional lenders. These "Participating Lenders" as they are called, each agree to loan a certain amount of money according to guidelines issued by the Housing Division. The loans are then purchased by the Housing Divison, with the bond sale funds.

Loans Are Not Available At All Times
Be aware that funds are not always available. There are frequent "dry spots" in between bond sales. If the money runs out and bonds can not be sold at rates low enough to provide loans at reasonable interest rates, the bond sale will be postponed.

A 5% down payment is the minimum allowed, although a larger down payment may be required depending upon the borrower's income and the sales price of the home. Mortgage insurance will be required on loans with a down payment of less than 25%.

Funds must be used by the Housing Division within a specified period, six months to one year of the bond sale. Sometimes there is a great demand for the loans and the supply is quickly exhausted. At other times, funds are available throughout the lending period.

The Housing Division intends to provide loans at lower-than-conventional rates, but occasionally these good intentions are foiled. Immediately after one bond sale within the last few years, interest rates on conventional loans dropped sharply, leaving the Housing Division's money unattractively expensive. Those funds were available for quite some time.

Who Is Eligible?
Both personal eligibility requirements and loan guidelines change very frequently in this program. Facts and figures quoted today could change within weeks. Fortunately, the general limits do not vary drastically, but if you are interested in this financing, ask a participating lender for the latest guidelines.

You may be eligible for a loan if:
- — you are an Oregon resident
- — your annual gross household income does not exceed the median income for the state (now $28,500*)
- — you have not owned a home within the last three years (except if you are purchasing a home in a target area, see below)
- — you will occupy the home as your permanent residence
- — the purchase price of the property does not exceed $65,000*

* subject to change

Loan Conditions And Terms
Loans are available for newly constructed or existing single-family houses, condominiums, townhouses and mobile homes with permanent foundations. The terms

112

on these fixed-rate loans are from 15 to 30 years for site-built homes, 20 years for single-wide mobile homes and 30 years for double-wide. Refinancing a home is not permitted.

Target Areas
There are certain areas throughout the state which have been designated as Target Areas, with the hope of increasing real estate activity in these locations. For a loan on property within a Target Area, it is permissible for a borrower to have owned property during the last three years.

Qualifying For A Loan
In determining if a borrower qualifies for the loan, lenders use the conventional method outlined in the chapter on qualifying for a loan. Follow the instructions given, using 28% on the Housing Cost Ratio, to see if you might be a likely candidate.

Buydown Plans
Temporary buydowns are available if the individual participating lenders choose to offer them. Although the guidelines for buydowns are subject to change, the program recently included a choice of graduated buydowns, from one to three years in duration.

Assumability Of The Loan
Single Family Mortgage Purchase Program loans are assumable at the original interest rate. The conditions that must be met, however, are so stringent that sellers often have difficulty finding a buyer who is able to satisfy all of the requirements.

In general, to assume any loan made after September 15, 1982, the new buyer must meet the eligibility requirements outlined for new loans. The current limitation on property price also applies to the resale price, if the loan is to be assumed. In addition, there are certain restrictions on second mortgages or trust deeds. Because these are owner-occupied home loans, a seller must obtain permission from the lender if he or she wishes to rent the home on a month-to-month basis while making a good faith effort to sell it.

Where To Apply For A Loan

Several major lending institutions and some smaller ones throughout the state are participating lenders. The list changes with each bond sale. It is necessary to contact one of these participating lenders directly if you wish to apply for a Mortgage Purchase Program loan. For names of participating lenders, contact:

Department of Commerce, Housing Division
110 Labor & Industries Building
Salem, OR 97310-0161

Phone: (503) 378-4343

Mortgage Credit Certificate Program (MCC)

Oregon homebuyers whose gross household income does not exceed the state median may qualify for a federal income tax credit upon purchase of a new or existing home, condominium, or manufactured home to be used as a principal residence. MCCs are also available for rehabilitation and home improvement loans. The tax credit, to up to 20 percent of the total annual interest on the loan, is available with conventional, FHA, VA loans, as well as privately insured loans and seller contracts. The home must not exceed these maximum prices (subject to change):

	NEW CONSTRUCTION		EXISTING RESIDENCE	
	Target area	Non-Target	Target area	Non-Target
Portland	$112,680	$103,290	$105,120	$ 96,360
Rest of Oregon	86,400	79,200	83,640	76,670

Contact a real estate agent or participating lender for assistance.

ADVANTAGES OF SINGLE FAMILY MORTGAGE PURCHASE PROGRAM
1. Excellent interest rate.
2. Easier to qualify for than conventional financing (at a higher rate of interest).

DISADVANTAGES OF SINGLE FAMILY MORTGAGE PURCHASE PROGRAM
1. Funds available sporadically.
2. Limited assumability.
3. Low sales price limit plus moderate income limit.

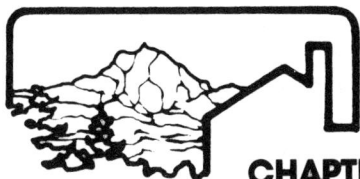

CHAPTER 16

FmHA Loans

DEFINITION: **Loans provided and subsidized by the Federal Government for the purchase of homes in rural areas by low- to moderate-income buyers.**

If your family income is low enough to meet the guidelines for this financing, and if you are looking for a modest home in a rural area or in a small country town, an FmHA loan may be just right for you.

The Farmers Home Administration is an agency of the U.S. Department of Agriculture. It offers a very wide range of credit programs to provide funds for rural projects that might be difficult to finance otherwise. The list is amazingly varied: in addition to home loans, there are loans for buying a farm, developing and conserving soil and water resources, forming a grazing association, building housing for farm laborers, and many other worthwhile projects. Here we are concerned with home financing and so we'll deal just with that particular area.

Home Financing

FmHA has two home loan programs, one for low-income borrowers, the other for moderate-income applicants. At the time of this publication, there is no money available for financing homes through the moderate income program and agency spokesmen do not know when, if ever, it will be funded. (However, some money is available to moderate-income borrowers for repairs to homes that are currently financed by FmHA).

Applications are being accepted for the low-income financing, although there is often a waiting list for available funds in many counties. This program offers a subsidized Interest Credit (I.C.) to borrowers whose income is too low to qualify for the regular monthly payment. The I.C. subsidy will reduce the monthly payment to a level that the buyer can afford, but the amount of the reduction will be added to the balance of the loan. That means it will eventually be repaid by the borrower when the home is sold.

FmHA loans are fixed-rate loans with a maximum term of 33 years. They are funded by the sale of notes to investors and therefore the interest rate on the loans depends upon the interest rates paid to these investors. In general, the rates on the loans are lower than standard market rates, with the I.C. subsidy providing even more favorable terms for those borrowers who qualify.

No down payment is required, except for any earnest money the seller might ask for. In other words, FmHA will finance up to 100% of the value of the home.

Who Is Eligible?
Maximum income limits are set by the FmHA and are strictly followed. However, 'Adjusted Income' is used rather than straight income. Here is how to calculate your Adjusted Income:

Take the total gross income (before taxes and deductions) of all the people who are living in the home. Subtract $480 for each minor child residing in the household and an additional $400 if the applicant or co-applicant is elderly, handicapped or disabled. Applicants or co-applicants 62 years of age or older may deduct that portion of their medical expenses exceeding 3% of their gross annual income. The FmHA may allow you to also subtract the cost of certain job-related expenses, such as child-care costs. The amount remaining is your Adjusted Income.

Example: A family with a gross income of $20,000, two dependent children and a handicapped applicant:

Gross Income . . . . $20,000.
Less $480 per child ($480 x 2) . . . . - 960.
Less $400 (disabled applicant) . . . . - 400.

Adjusted Income . . . . $18,640.

To qualify for a loan, the applicant's Adjusted Income must not exceed the limits set by FmHA. These limits vary with the location of the home and the number of household members.

As an example, the maximum Adjusted Income for a family of four ranges from $14,900 in some counties, to $24,100 in others. The family in our example above would qualify for a loan only in those counties with a limit of $18,640 or higher. 40% of all available funds are allocated for what are known as Very Low Income Loans, with these maximum income limits for a family of four ranging from $10,800 to $15,050, depending upon the county where the home is located.

Which Homes Are Eligible?
The FmHA county offices have maps showing which areas are eligible for loans. These are strictly open country areas or rural towns with a population of 10,000 or less (or up to 20,000, if not in a 'metropolitan statistical area', close to a city). Bedroom communities or suburbs are not eligible.

The homes themselves must be adequate to meet the needs of the family but modest in size, design and cost. A 1000 square foot, three-bedroom home with a garage is typical of the type financed by the FmHA. Any extras that are not absolutely essential, such as additional bathrooms, family rooms or daylight basements usually will not be approved.

The lot must be of a modest size also and is limited to approximately one acre. FmHA does finance farms, too, and questions concerning these loans should be directed to the local FmHA office.

If you wish to have a home built, you may secure permanent financing through FmHA, but you must obtain a temporary construction loan from another source. You must find your own builder and have a set of plans available for the administration to approve. Mobile homes may not be financed.

Where To Apply
You must apply for a loan at the FmHA office that serves the county in which the home is located. There are 19 offices throughout Oregon, most of them covering two or even three counties. To find the office you

need, look in the phone book under the U.S. Department of Agriculture or contact a State or District Field Office below.

FmHA State Office:
Room 1590, Federal Building,
1220 SW 3rd,
Portland, OR 97204
Phone: (503) 221-2734

District 1 includes the following counties: Baker, Crook, Deschutes, Gilliam, Grant, Harney, Jefferson, Malheur, Morrow, Umatilla, Union, Wallowa, Wheeler

FmHA Field Office, District 1
225 SW First Avenue,
Ontario, OR 97914
Phone: (503) 889-7609

District 2 includes the following counties: Clackamas, Clatsop, Columbia, Hood River, Marion, Multnomah, Polk, Sherman, Tillamook, Wasco, Washington and Yamhill.

FmHA Field Office, District 2
16770 SE 82nd Drive,
Clackamas, OR 97015
Phone: (503) 655-7185

District 3 includes the following counties: Benton, Coos, Curry, Douglas, Jackson, Josephine, Klamath, Lake, Lane, Lincoln and Linn.

FmHA Field Office, District 3
Room 242, Federal Building,
211 E. 7th Street,
Eugene, OR 97401
Phone: (503) 687-6850

ADVANTAGES OF FARMERS HOME ADMINSTRATION LOANS

1. Low interest rates.
2. Payment subsidy for low-income borrowers.
3. Up to 100% loan-to-value ratio.

DISADVANTAGES OF FARMERS HOME ADMINISTRATION LOANS

1. Low-income borrowers only may receive financing at this time.
2. The home must be modest in size and amenities.
3. It must be located in a designated rural area.

Part IV

Seller-Financing

DEFINITION: Seller Financing is an agreement between the buyer and seller of a piece of property. Instead of receiving a cash payment for the equity at the time of sale, the seller agrees to accept a series of partial payments or full payment at a later date.

Whenever interest rates are high, seller financing leaps out of the shadows, clad in a bright red Superhero cape. Buyers and sellers cheer. Real estate agents order more 'Sold' signs. Attorneys sharpen their pencils. The word gets around: seller financing is here to save Oregon from the woes of outrageous interest rates, qualifying difficulties, and impossible loan fees.

There is no doubt that seller financing has been a boon to real estate in recent years. Thousands of Oregon homes would never have been sold if the sellers themselves had not funded the transaction, either wholly or partially. It has been interesting to watch the public's acceptance grow, from skepticism to contract-mania. Thank goodness we have finally settled in to a level somewhere between the two!

Seller financing should neither be avoided, nor given superhero status. Like any other financing method, it does an excellent job in some situations. Yet even when interest rates are soaring and loans are difficult to obtain, a contract is not always the best way to finance a home. Study the pros and cons, as well as other financing possibilities, before making a decison.

Types Of Seller Financing Commonly Used

There are two different seller financing methods that are frequently used in Oregon home sales: the land sales contract and the second deed of trust. Other forms make an occasional apperance at the hands of an attorney, but they are used so rarely that we will skip over them with just a brief mention. For additional creative techniques to use with seller financing, study Part V, dealing with Assumptions and Miscellaneous Financing.

CHAPTER 17

Land Sales Contracts

DEFINITION: **A Land Sales Contract is an agreement between the buyer and seller of a piece of property. It differs from other forms of seller financing in that the seller usually retains legal title to the property until the buyer has made the final payment.**

You may have heard Land Sales Contracts called "land contracts", "contracts for deed" or just plain "contracts". Even though contract sales have become very popular in the past few years, the idea is not a new one. People have been buying and selling homes on contract for centuries. Today the process has been refined, and there are laws which offer guidelines and protection for both parties.

How A Contract Works

Let's use an imaginary situation to illustrate a contract sale:

The Smiths' home is for sale. Dottie and Roger are asking $62,500. Two real estate agents show the home one day and both prospective buyers write offers to buy. (I did warn you that this was a figment of my imagination!) The agents explain each offer to the Smiths.

Offer number one is an all cash offer of $55,000. The second offer is for $61,000. It offers $10,000 in cash as a down payment and asks the Smiths to carry a contract in the amount of $51,000 at 12% interest for 30 years. Which should the Smiths consider?

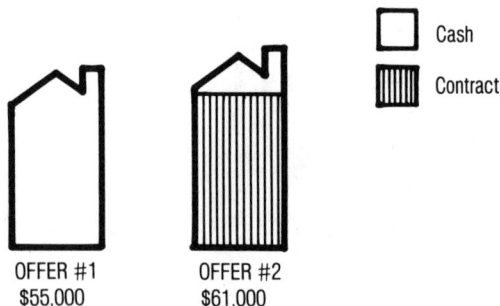

Cash

Contract

OFFER #1
$55,000

OFFER #2
$61,000

WHICH OFFER SHOULD THE SMITHS CONSIDER?

Offer number one is a simple transaction. At closing, the buyers would pay cash, closing expenses would be paid and the Smiths would receive the balance. They would give possession and legal title to the buyers and would have no further legal interest in the home.

Offer number two is for a higher price, as many contract transactions are, since the seller will be acting as lender. However, the Smiths would receive less cash at closing. Here the buyers and the sellers would enter into a contract agreement, drawn up by an attorney and signed by both parties. The buyers would pay the $10,000 cash plus their closing expenses. The sellers' closing costs and broker's fees would be deducted from the $10,000 and the balance would go to the Smiths.

According to the terms of the contract agreement, the new buyers would pay the Smiths $525 a month in principal and interest, and would pay the taxes and insurance when due. They would take possession of the home but would not receive legal title, the deed to the property, until the last payment has been made. This explains the term "contract for deed"; the buyer and seller enter into an agreement to transfer the deed when the contract terms have been met.

Dottie and Roger will have to decide whether to accept (or counter) the all-cash offer or to accept the contract offer with its small amount of cash at closing plus 12% return on the money they have invested in their home. They will base their decision on many factors. Do they need cash to buy another home? Is 12% a reasonable interest rate to earn? Is one offer better than the other from a tax standpoint? Are the buyers reliable?

No Such Thing As A "Standard" Contract

An important thing to remember is that a contract is a collection of points that both the buyer and seller agree to follow. A contract between the Smiths and the buyers may include provisions that other buyers and sellers would not want to have included. For example, the buyers may wish to have a statement included that allows the contract to be assumed by a new buyer if they should decide to sell. If the Smiths are in agreement, fine. If not, the sale cannot take place until a compromise has been reached.

Seek Professional Advice

You can, if you wish, walk into an office supply store and buy a blank contract form. There may be several varieties to choose from, each with a dizzying spread of small print and large words. But I cannot over-emphasize the importance of good legal advice for any contract sale. One local attorney told me that the blank contract forms often favor the rights of one party over another. If you aren't sure just what your rights are, can you recognize when they have been overlooked?

A competent attorney may choose to use a blank form, or may type up a different version, but you can be sure that the end result will protect your interest in the property. Most attorneys charge from $100 to $200 to draw up a simple real estate contract. Either the buyer or the seller may pay for the preparation, however the other party should ask his or her own attorney to review the contract after it is written and before it is signed.

Contract Provisions

There are many provisions which should be included in a contract and others that are optional. It is wise to have the contract provisions also written into the original sales agreement (the offer to buy the property), although they can be added at the time the contract is prepared if both parties agree.

Some provisions will appear in all contracts: the size, frequency and duration of the monthly payments, or how and when the taxes and insurance are to be paid. There should be default provisions, outlining a plan of action if either party fails to keep the agreement. In addition, there will be an agreement to convey the deed to the buyer at a specific time, usually when the final payment has been made.

The following provisions are optional but are often used in contracts:

Balloon payment: A balloon payment is a lump-sum payment of the principal amount. If the Smiths, in our example above, did not want to carry the contract for 30 years, they would have two options. First, they could amortize the payments over a shorter period of time, for instance, 15 years, increasing the monthly payments from $525 to $612. That would be fine for the Smiths but it might be impossible for the buyers to pay that amount.

The second option is to add a balloon payment provision to the original offer. The payments could be amortized over a 30-year period, with payments of $525, but at the end of 15 years, the entire remaining loan balance would be due. In this case, $43,710 out of the original $51,000 would be owed to the Smiths. That means that the buyers would have to come up with $43,710 in cash to pay off the loan. Usually this is done by refinancing the home.

What happens if the buyers cannot get financing? As Shakespeare put it, "Ay, there's the rub". What does happen depends entirely upon the wording of the contract. Many contracts give the seller the right to start foreclosure proceedings and the buyer could lose the property. But with some extra preparation at the time the contract is drawn up, this problem can be eased a bit. The following provision deals with this.

Extension Provision: This escape clause gives the buyer extra time to refinance the home or to sell it to a new buyer who can obtain a loan. There are many ways to word an extension provision, to the satisfaction of both the buyer and seller, but in general, it provides a contract extension of 6 months or a year if the buyer has been unable to refinance. There may be an increase in interest rate and monthly payments during the extension, in order to encourage the buyer to keep trying.

Assumption Provision: Most buyers would love to have the right to let a new buyer assume the contract. That could increase the salability of the home considerably. Many sellers, however, want to have some say in the matter. They do not want to find themselves locked into a contract with a new buyer who cannot really afford the home.

An assumption provision outlines the rules that both parties agree to follow. Will an assumption be permitted, or must the contract be paid off when the home is sold? Will the interest rate remain the same upon assumption? How will the new buyer's credit worthiness be determined? If the answers to these questions are included in the contract, both parties know exactly where they stand.

Determining A Fair Rate Of Interest

An offer to buy a home on contract should mention all of the specific details that are to be included in the contract. While real estate agents are not attorneys and cannot give you legal advice, they can be very helpful in suggesting market trends. They will be able to tell you what interest rates local sellers are charging and what provisions are customarily included.

Contracts usually carry a lower interest rate than institutional loans. That, after all, is the primary purpose of seller financing: to provide affordable financing when it is not available elsewhere. As compensation for the seller, contract sales usually command a higher sales price than a sale involving an outside lender. Your real estate agent can help you determine a reasonable price, based upon other comparable sales.

Imputed Interest And The IRS

Sellers may wish to ask the advice of a tax accountant, too, before agreeing to sell a home on contract. The IRS follows an imputed interest rule that has been the subject of heated debates in Congress. If a seller offers a contract at an interest rate lower than the rate set by the government (currently 9% but subject to change), the IRS will impute, or attribute, a higher interest rate to the transaction for tax purposes. (That higher rate is currently 10% but also subject to change.)

In other words, sellers who enter into contracts at 7% or 8% interest, for example, will be taxed as though they had received 10% interest. Congress has toyed with tough new imputed interest levels, but so far home sales (at least those under two million dollars!) have escaped unscathed. Check with an accountant or the IRS to be certain.

Can A Contract Be Used With An Existing Loan

A home with an existing loan may be bought or sold on contract provided there is no due-on-sale clause in the original loan agreement. (A due-on-sale clause requires that the loan be paid in full when the property is sold.) There may also be some conditions set by the lender, which must be followed in the case of a contract sale.

In the example above, the Smiths' home is free and clear. There is no underlying loan that might have prevented them from selling their home on contract. Let us suppose instead that there is a loan, with a current balance of $31,000. Here is how the second offer would look, in the form of a chart:

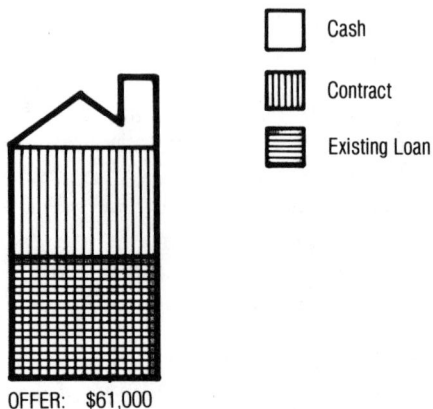

☐ Cash

▥ Contract

▤ Existing Loan

OFFER: $61,000

A CONTRACT WITH AN EXISTING LOAN

126

From the buyer's point of view, nothing has changed. The contract is still in the amount of $51,000, at 12% interest and with monthly payments of $525, principal and interest. The existing loan would remain in the sellers' names and they would continue to make their monthly payments as before. Therefore the Smiths' net monthly income would be $525, less the amount paid to the original lender.

Lender's Permission To Sell On Contract
If your home, or the one you wish to buy, has an existing loan, contact the lender to find out whether or not it may be sold on contract. Most real estate agents routinely secure this information in writing from the lender at the time the home is put on the market. While some institutions will give you an answer over the telephone, many require a letter signed by the borrower, instructing them to release the information. Be sure to include the loan number for a prompt reply.

Most real estate agents have form letters to send to lending institutions when the home is listed. It's a good time to inquire about the assumability of the loan also and to notify your lender that you plan to sell your home. Ask for a written confirmation and save it. The buyer as well as the seller should keep a copy. One client of mine agreed to sell his home on contract, but before closing, his savings and loan was purchased by another institution with very different policies. Sincer we had a written confirmation from the first institution, the new lender reluctantly agreed to abide by the old rules. Without it, my client would have been charged an additional $700.

Here Is What You'll Need To Know:
1. May this home be sold on contract?
2. If so, will the interest rate be increased at the time of sale?
3. Must the contract be approved or the buyer qualified by your department?
4. Is the loan assumable?
5. If so, at what interest rate may it be assumed?
6. May the seller carry a second trust deed?
7. Must the buyer qualify for an assumption?

8. What fee do you charge for a contract sale? For an assumption?
9. If the home is sold on contract, may the loan later be assumed?
10. Will the interest rate be increased again?
11. How long will it take you to approve the documents or process an assumption?
12. For how long will this information be valid?

If there is an existing second or third mortgage loan, contact each lender and ask the same questions.

What If The Answer Is "No"?

Never go behind a lender's back and enter into a contract sale without written approval. Lending institutions have those same extrasensory powers developed by mothers of small children. They know everything. Or at least, they'll inevitably find out, and the consequences can be disastrous.

What can happen? If you proceed with the contract sale without the lender's approval, many or most loan documents give the lender the right to call the loan. In other words, the loan must be repaid in full immediately. If you do not have the cash on hand, you may find it difficult to scratch up another loan on the spur of the moment. The lender can proceed with foreclosure and the buyer could lose the home.

In spite of these serious consequences, many borrowers have gambled. I have heard these words so often, "This is a big city, the bank'll never find out." Don't count on it! Lenders can and do unearth these clandestine transactions with little apparent effort. When the seller cancels the homeowner's insurance policy and the buyer replaces it, the lending institution is notified. County tax records are a giveaway, as are courthouse files, where the contract is recorded. At the height of the contract-mania in recent years, when interest rates were extremely high, one loan officer told me that his firm made an effort to spotcheck loan accounts for this very practice.

How "Safe" Are Contract Sales?

There is an element of risk in any transaction, but buyers and sellers alike get nervous when there is no lending institution to run the show. Sellers fear that the buyers who seemed like good solid American citizens at closing will turn into slovenly deadbeats the following month. Buyers are afraid that they will discover, a week after the contract has been recorded, that the fresh wallpaper in the hall covered a termite jamboree.

Take a lesson from the institutional lenders; these things occasionally happen to them too. They lessen the problem by careful checking of both the borrower and the property before making the loan. While the institutions have professional advisors on staff or on call, buyers and sellers can do their own legwork or hire independent help.

Sellers can and should request that the buyers submit a credit information form before the offer is accepted. This form is similar to a loan application form used by a lending institution. A blank may be obtained from your real estate agent or from an office supply store that stocks legal forms. Financial and personal references provided by the buyers may be contacted and assessed.

The preliminary title report, prepared by the company providing title insurance, will indicate any judgments against either buyers or sellers, and will show existing liens against the property. (Learn more about this in the chapter on Escrow Closing.) These facts are gathered by the title insurance company from county courthouse records.

As for the quality and condition of the property itself, buyers should make a thorough inspection and should hire professional inspectors if they have any doubts or questions. In some areas of the state, there are companies that will check an entire home for a reasonable fee and will give a written report of the findings. Individual parts of a home, such as the roof, plumbing, electrical system, heating system and structure, may be inspected by separate contractors hired by the buyer.

129

Sometimes a boundary survey seems warranted if the property lines are in question.

Do not be afraid to satisfy any doubts before closing. It is common practice for a buyer to make an offer that is contingent upon his or her approval of the inspection results. If the offer is accepted and the inspection shows the need for repair, the buyer may accept the situation or negotiate with the seller for the costs.

The fair value of the home is another question that arises. Lending institutions hire appraisers to evaluate the property before they make a loan. Contract buyers may do the same, if they have doubts about the purchase price. For a single family home, an appraisal of this type will cost around $175. As an alternative, your real estate agent can provide information about recent comparable sales to help determine the fair market value.

A Buyer And A Property That Are Less Than Perfect
With all these precautions and a well-written contract, the risks in a contract sale can easily be kept under control. But that does not mean that a buyer who is a little shaky in the credit department is automatically ruled out. Sellers can be very understanding people and are often willing to be more flexible than an institutional lender.

Bankruptcy is a good example. It is difficult for a person who has declared bankruptcy, expecially within recent years, to obtain institutional financing. Lenders have rules that are difficult to bend, even if the circumstances are unusual. A seller, however, might be willing to overlook the bankruptcy and concentrate, for example, on the recent spotless years and an excellent new job.

Self-employed buyers or those who have been employed for less than two years may find it easier to buy on contract, since institutions like to see a proven, steady income track record.

Similarly, a home that is not up to snuff by bank standards might be perfectly acceptable to a buyer who understands the problems. For example, a house without a permanent foundation is difficult, if not impossible, to finance conventionally. So is a modest home on an unusually large parcel of property in a residential neighborhood. Both of these would be excellent candidates for contract sales.

Monthly Payment Collection
Buyers and sellers sometimes worry about the handling of the monthly payment. Who calculates the amount that is to be credited toward interest and principal, since those change each month? Many lending institutions and some escrow companies provide a service known as an Escrow Collection Account or a Contract Collection Account. For a set-up fee ($50 to $75) and a small monthly service fee ($5 and up), they will receive the payment from the buyer each month, deposit it and issue a check to the seller. At the end of each year, a written accounting of principal and interest is sent to each party. Arrangements may be made for the payment of an underlying loan, directly from the collection account. This service does not act as a collection agency, pressuring buyers into paying; it simply processes funds as instructed by the contract.

Preparing The Deed
When the last payment has been made, the seller will give the buyer a deed to the property. If the seller has moved to Pago Pago or is on a round-the-world balloon expedition, the deed may not be forthcoming. That is why many buyers and sellers choose to have the deed prepared at closing and held by a neutral party until needed. A Contract Collection Account often includes this service, or an attorney may do so.

Selling A Contract
If a seller needs cash at closing and the buyer's down payment seems all too small, it is possible for the seller to sell the contract for a cash payment. Plans should be made at the time the offer is written, so that the terms of the contract will be attractive to a contract buyer. To find out more about selling a contract or a note, read the chapter in the section on Assumptions & Miscellaneous Financing that deals with this.

Recording The Contract
In Oregon, any contract that will be in effect more than one year must be recorded by the seller within 15 days after signing. The escrow agent will see that it is properly recorded in the county where the home is located. Recording protects the buyer's official claim to the property and should not be overlooked.

ADVANTAGES OF A CONTRACT SALE
1. Seller may offer a lower-than-market interest rate and better terms.
2. Buyer does not necessarily have to meet institutional lending qualifying standards.
3. Property condition does not have to meet institutional standards, if buyer agrees.
4. Seller receives a monthly income, including interest on the equity.

DISADVANTAGES OF A CONTRACT SALE
1. Seller does not receive the total equity in cash at closing.
2. Seller is absorbing some of the risk that the lender normally takes.
3. A poorly written contract can be unpleasant or disastrous for both parties.

CHAPTER 18

Seller-Financed Second Deed Of Trust

DEFINITION: With this financing method, the buyer assumes the seller's existing loan (or obtains a new loan) and gives the seller a note secured by a trust deed, for the amount not covered by the down payment and the loan.

This is a popular method of owner financing in situations where there is an existing loan that is assumable. It is used less frequently with new loans, for reasons I will mention later.

To see how it looks in chart form, let's go back to the last example in the chapter on contracts. If you remember, the Smiths received an offer of $61,000 for their home. The buyers had a down payment of $10,000 and asked the Smiths to carry a contract for the balance, $51,000. The existing $31,000 loan would stay in the Smiths' names.

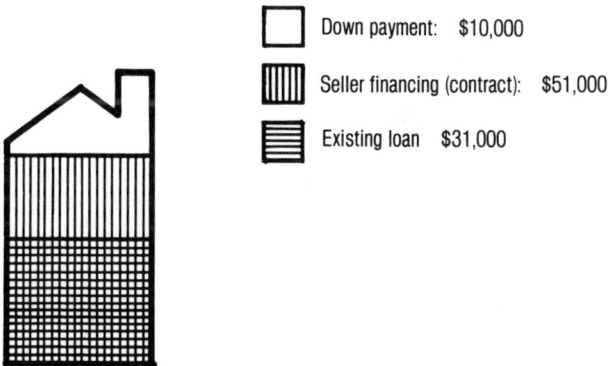

Down payment: $10,000

Seller financing (contract): $51,000

Existing loan $31,000

A CONTRACT SALE

This same situation could be financed differently. The buyers could assume the existing $31,000 loan, with the lender's permission. (Learn more about assumptions in a later chapter.) The down payment would still be $10,000. But instead of a contract in the amount of $51,000, the Smiths would carry a note, secured by a second deed of trust, in the amount of only $20,000.

Other than the down payment, no funds would change hands at closing. The Smiths would receive the $20,000 plus interest, according to their agreement with the buyers. For instance, the two parties might agree to fully amortized monthly payments over a number of years. Or perhaps they would prefer monthly payments with a balloon payment on a certain date. For some buyers and sellers, large yearly payments would be best. The size and distribution of payments is limited only by the imagination and willingness of both parties.

No matter what agreement is reached, the buyers are responsible for two separate payments: one to the original lender, the other to the Smiths. Here is how it looks:

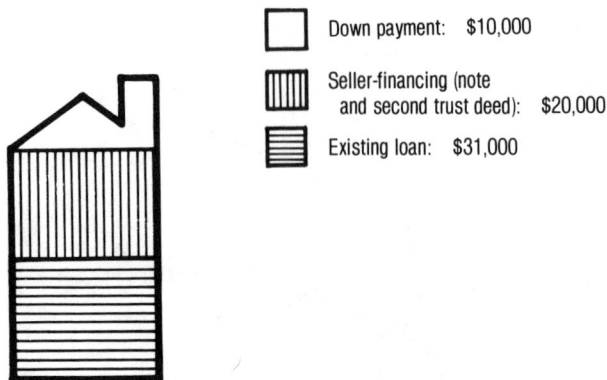

Down payment: $10,000

Seller-financing (note and second trust deed): $20,000

Existing loan: $31,000

AN ASSUMPTION PLUS SELLER-FINANCED SECOND

"Notes" And "Trust Deeds" Explained

To understand the differences between a contract sale and an assumption with a second trust deed, you will need to know what the terms mean. Notes and trust deeds are not just used in seller financing. They are standard financing documents also used by lending institutions for their real estate loans.

A "note", or "promissory note", is a document which describes the debt and the borrower's promise to pay that debt. A buyer will sign the note, but will also give the seller collateral, or security, to back that promise. In real estate, that security is the property itself.

A "trust deed", or "deed of trust" is the document that gives the lender (in this case the seller) a legal interest in the property, equal to the amount of the debt. The two documents, the note and the trust deed, go hand in hand.

Why Not A "Second Mortgage"?

A "mortgage" is similar to a trust deed in that it is also security for a note. We often hear the words "second mortgage". However most lenders prefer to use the trust deed because foreclosure on a trust deed is a shorter, easier procedure. Mortgages are rarely used in Oregon today.

Preparation Of The Documents

Standard notes and trust deed are not complicated to draw up. An escrow agent can prepare them, usually without additional charge, while working on all the other closing papers. You may ask for a copy of both in advance if you wish to study them or have your attorney look at them.

Why This Is A "Second" Trust Deed

The difference between a "first" and a "second" trust deed is not in the documents themselves but in the order in which they are recorded in the county files. The first loan on a home will be the "first mortgage loan" or the "first trust deed loan". A loan or note and trust deed recorded later would be a "second mortgage loan" or "second trust deed". An even later recording would be a "third trust deed", and so on. This is known as the "lien position". If the loan in first position is paid off, then the remaining loans move up a notch. The second trust deed now becomes a first trust deed; the third trust deed becomes a second.

The position of the trust deed is important if a foreclosure is necessary. After a foreclosure sale, funds received are used to reimburse the lenders in the order in which the loans were recorded. The first trust deed loan would be paid in full before the holder of the second trust deed receives any money.

In the example above, the Smiths are in second position, whether they carry a contract or a second deed of trust. Therefore, in a foreclosure sale, the underlying $31,000 loan would be paid first. Next the Smiths would receive payment for their note if funds are available.

Seller-Financed Trust Deeds With A New Loan
Occasionally a seller is asked to carry a second deed of trust on top of a new institutional loan secured by the buyer. Many conventional and government lenders do not allow this; those that do insist that the sum of the payments on both loans be considered in determining whether or not the buyer is qualified. (See the chapter on Qualifying For A Loan.) Unless the monthly payments on the second are much lower than those on a similar-sized institutional loan, a buyer who is unable to qualify for the full amount owed will not be helped by seller financing.

IRS And Imputed Interest
The Internal Revenue's imputed interest rule applies to all seller-financing, whether it be a contract or a note-and-trust deed. Read the section about imputed interest in the chapter on Contracts and consult your tax accountant or the IRS for current rates.

Using An Escrow Collection Account
The Escrow Collection Account (also known as a Contract Collection Account) that was discussed in the last chapter may be used with second trust deed financing also, if buyer and seller agree. This should be discussed at the time the offer is made.

Contracts vs. Seller-Financed Seconds

Should a seller who is willing to finance the sale of a home choose a contract or an assumption with a second trust deed? Would a buyer be better to assume the loan or to buy on contract? There are no standard answers for these questions. Each situation brings different requirements, but by studying the pros and cons of each method, the best solution usually becomes apparent. Your attorney may offer suggestions to help you decide.

Assumability Of The Existing Loan

One deciding factor may be the assumability of the existing loan. Use the questionnaire in the chapter on contracts to find out whether or not the loan may be assumed and if the home may be sold on contract. Study all the information carefully. Will the interest rates increase for either or both types of financing? What fees are involved? If the home is sold on contract, may the loan later be assumed? At what cost? Must the buyer be approved by the lender for a contract as well as an assumption?

Often the answers to these questions will make one of the two financing methods seem more attractive. Lenders generally, but not always, have more demanding requirements for an assumption, since a seller who carries a contract absorbs some of the risk. Here are other points to mull over as you make a decision.

The Matter Of Foreclosure

Foreclosure is not a nice thing to consider but sellers especially are wise to be aware of the consequences.

Let's look at contracts first. With a contract sale, the responsibility for an underlying loan remains with the sellers. They must continue to make the monthly loan payments, even if the buyers miss a contract payment. Failure to do so may result in foreclosure proceedings, brought by the original lender against the sellers. (There is a clause in most contracts that permits buyers to make payments on the underlying loan, directly to the original lender, if the seller neglects to do so. This gives buyers an opportunity to prevent a foreclosure from occurring through no fault of their own.)

If the buyers do not abide by the terms of the contract, the sellers may seek foreclosure through court action. In most cases, this results in a return of the property to the seller, although the court may order a foreclosure sale if the buyer has considerable equity in the property.

With the other method, an assumption plus a seller-financed second trust deed, the buyers are responsible for making both payments. If they fail to do so, either lender (the original lender or the seller) may institute foreclosure proceedings. The property will be sold in a foreclosure sale and the loans will be paid off in their recorded order. The property will not be returned to the seller.

ADVANTAGES OF A
SELLER-FINANCED SECOND

1. Seller may offer an excellent interest rate and terms.
2. Buyer may find it easier to qualify for this financing than for a new loan, if interest rates on the assumption and second are lower.
3. Seller receives an income from the investment.
4. Seller is relieved of responsibility of making payments on the underlying loan.
5. If foreclosure is necessary, lender in first position may institute proceedings. (This is a disadvantage if seller does not want a foreclosure.)

DISADVANTAGES OF A
SELLER-FINANCED SECOND

1. There is a certain amount of risk in any seller financing.
2. The seller does not receive all the equity in cash at closing.
3. In a foreclosure, the seller will not receive the property, unless he or she purchases it at the foreclosure sale. (This may be considered an advantage!)

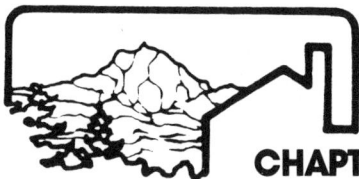

CHAPTER 19

Other Types Of
Seller-Financing

The two kinds of seller financing we have covered are by far the most commonly used. Once in awhile, escrow agents see a variation on the theme, usually under the masterful direction of an attorney. There are rare occasions, since the standard techniques work well for financing a home in Oregon. However I will mention them in passing, so that you will be aware of their existence.

Trust Deeds And Mortgages
The last chapter dealt with second trust deeds in combination with an assumption or a new loan. But a note and trust deed (or a note and mortgage) may be used by a seller in the same way that a lending institution does, as the primary financing technique in situations where the property is owned free and clear. In other words, if there is no existing loan on the property, the seller may have the buyer sign a note secured by a trust deed on the home.

According to attorneys, these documents are occasionally used instead of a land sales contract because of the difference in foreclosure procedures between the two, as outlined briefly in the last chapter. Another point of difference is the disposition of title to the property. In a land sales contract, the seller usually retains legal title until the final payment has been made. This is not true of a trust deed or mortgage.

All-Inclusive Trust Deed (AITD)

Oregon had a brief fling with all-inclusive trust deeds but the romance faded almost as quickly as it appeared. An AITD is a form of trust deed that was designed to be used with an underlying loan, in much the same method as a contract. Again, the main differences between the two lie in the areas of foreclosure and title.

Your decision to use a particular form of seller financing should be made with legal counsel. This book can only describe what is commonly done in Oregon; your attorney can prescribe what is best for you.

Part V

Assumptions And Miscellaneous Financing

This section gathers together all of the assorted techniques which inhabit the realm of creative financing. Here we find a host of handy little ideas to use when interest rates are unpalatably high, or when other methods, by themselves, cannot finance the whole house.

Assumptions have been included in this section, since they are the basis for so many innovative techniques. Excellent assumptions are hard to find these days and good assumptions often need the assistance of secondary financing. Suggestions for putting together a package of money ideas will, I hope, inspire successful transactions.

Since I started writing this book, I have had several requests for "no money down" tips. Television seminars promise unlimited wealth and opportunity through real estate, without investing a penny (except, of course, the $297 for their trade secrets). It sounds terribly easy! The truth is, purchasing property with no money down is not at all impossible, but may not be practical or desirable for many homebuyers. You will have to make that decision for yourself after studying the "No Money Down" chapter in this section. While I cannot give you one magic key for every no-cash purchase, I can steer you in the right direction and offer practical strategies.

Here, then, is a grab-bag of home financing tricks and treats. Good luck!

CHAPTER 20

Assumptions

DEFINITION: **In an assumption, the seller's existing loan is transferred to the buyer, who will then assume responsibility for making the monthly payments.**

Just when we need a good old-fashioned assumption, the creek has dried to a trickle. Assumptions are wonderful financing tools when interest rates are unapproachably high. If buyers could assume existing loans at, for instance, 7% interest, who would bother applying for new loans at 15%? Almost no one, of course, and therein lies the problem. While this arrangement would delight the buyers and sellers, lending institutions would be hanging Out-Of-Business signs in their front windows.

Why There Are So Few Good Assumptions
We have had several years of unsteady interest rates. No one can accurately predict the upswings and downturns of the mortgage market, and lenders cannot afford to be caught off-guard. It is unprofitable for a lending institution to have an abundance of old, low-interest loans still on the books. Why earn 7% when a new loan would bring much higher interest?

Lenders tackled the problem in two ways. First, many wrote enticing letters to their borrowers, suggesting that they refinance their homes. "Receive cash for your equity!" the letters read. Some borrowers took the cash and traded their 7% or 8% loans for a new one at a higher rate.

The second target area was assumptions. Until the late seventies, many loans were readily assumable, at or near the original interest rate. Yet when new loans were easy to obtain and just a percent or two higher in interest than the existing loan, few buyers needed an assumption to afford a home. Now that new financing is considerably more expensive, good assumptions are very welcome. The trouble is, they are becoming harder to find. Today very few loans are assumable with no strings attached and many lenders do not allow their new loans to be assumed at all.

We cannot blame the lenders entirely for the shortage of good assumptions. The real estate boom of the 1970s played a part, too. During those years, property values increased at a feverish pace, often 15% or 20% a year. This meant that a home purchased in 1974 for $30,000 might be back on the market in 1980 for $70,000 or more. Even if the interest rate on the underlying 1974 loan were around 8% (a very attractive rate to assume), the loan balance would be down to $20,000 or $25,000. That would be of little help to the buyer in 1980. Since the home was by then worth $70,000, the buyer would have to finance or cash out the $45,000 to $50,000 difference. Although the existing loan might technically be assumable, it could certainly not be considered a "good" assumption.

Types Of Assumptions
In general, there are two types of assumptions: one where the seller is still held responsible to a certain degree, the other in which the seller is released from responsibility. The type used in a transaction depends on the wording of the original loan documents and the lender's current policy. Some lenders offer a choice; most do not.

If the lender requires the new buyer to make formal application and qualify for the loan, that may be an indication that the lender is willing to offer a release. Ask the lender to be certain. An assumption where the lender does not require a formal application and qualification, and where the assumption may be handled entirely by the escrow officer, is probably an assumption without a release of liability.

While the assumption-with-release sounds more appealing to a seller, the alternative, commonly known as a "simple assumption" or a "blind assumption" (because the lender does not need to see the new buyer) is more
144

attractive to a buyer. Blind assumptions are usually less expensive. There is no credit report to pay for and the assumption fee is often less. The best known simple assumptions are on FHA, VA, and DVA loans, although all also offer assumptions-with-release. Because of the low (or no) down payment required on FHA and VA loans, their loan balances are higher than conventional loans, creating better assumptions years later.

For buyers with a blemish on their credit record or insufficient income to qualify, blind assumptions are the perfect answer, provided the seller is willing to allow the assumption-without-release. As long as the buyer continues to make regular payments to the lender, the seller's liability will never come into play. But in the case of default by the buyer, the seller could be held responsible, to a certain degree. The seller in the following case history was concerned about this.

Case History: Mr. Meyer

One of my clients, a distinguished gentleman named Mr. Meyer, received an offer for his home. The buyer, a young woman in her mid-twenties, could not qualify for a new loan at the high interest rates available at that time. Instead, she offered to assume Mr. Meyer's existing low-interest loan.

When Mr. Meyer received the assumption information from his lender, he was worried. The loan was certainly assumable, that wasn't the problem. In fact it was a splendid blind assumption. There would be no increase in the interest rate, the buyer did not have to qualify for the loan and the lender did not even want to know the buyer's name until after the closing. But Mr. Meyer discovered that, according to the lender's policy, he would not be released from responsibility for the loan. He was concerned that the buyer would default and leave him to face the wrath of the lender. Even though this was the first offer Mr. Meyer had received for his home in six months, his first impulse was to reject it.

I suggested that he discuss the matter with his attorney, allowing the lawyer to review the original loan documents. The results were reassuring. According to the bank's assumption department, Mr. Meyer would remain in a position of liability. In a case of default by the buyer, the bank had outlined the steps it would take to recover its loss. First would come the foreclosure and sale, at which the home would go to the highest bidder. But what would happen if the foreclosure sale did not bring in a high enough offer to repay the lender? Mr. Meyer wondered if the bank would ask him to pay the difference.

The attorney could find nothing in the loan documents that would allow the lender to do this. In fact, disguised in legal jargon was a clause that specifically removed the lender's right to recover a loss in such a way. When this was explained to Mr. Meyer, he accepted the buyer's offer immediately.

Not all loan documents are created equal. Mr. Meyer was fortunate that his lender's announced policy differed from actual fact. Other loan documents may give a lender different rights in the matter of liability. Without a release, a seller may be required to reimburse the bank for a loss after foreclosure if the buyer is unable to pay. An attorney can give you an idea of the risks involved, if any.

Most of today's assumptions require the buyer to make formal application and to qualify for the assumption. To find out the lender's policies, send a letter to the institution, asking the questions outlined in the chapter on Contracts. This will give you a written record of the requirements, costs and time involved.

Assumption Fees
It is usually less expensive to assume a loan than to obtain a new one. The biggest saving lies in the fee itself. A fee for a new loan is often 3% or 4% of the loan amount; assumption fees rarely top 2% and are usually even less.

Other closing costs may be reduced for an assumption. This will be covered in detail in the chapter on Loan Fees And Closing Costs but here are some of the major points. Many lenders do not require an appraisal, since the home was appraised when they made the original loan. For some assumptions, primarily those without the seller's release of liability, it is not necessary for the buyer to pay for a credit report. In addition, the buyer saves the cost of a mortgagee's title insurance policy. The total amount saved by assuming a loan ranges from a few hundred to well over a thousand dollars.

The Interest Rate Question

Very few loans, except for certain government loans such as FHA and federal VA, are assumable at the original interest rate. Assumptions usually bring an increase. This change can be a minimal 1% or 2%, or it could be so great that it would discourage anyone from assuming the loan. For example, the rate on some loans changes to the current market rate if the loan is assumed. One lender routinely raises the interest to $\frac{1}{4}$ of 1% above the market rate. Even so, for some buyers, an assumption at these rates might still be preferable to a new loan.

Recalculating The Payments

If the interest rate on the loan is increased, the monthly payments will also increase. They must be recalculated at the higher rate. Also, they must be re-amortized over the remaining term of the loan, no longer thirty years, or fifteen years, or whatever its original lifespan was.

It is very easy to calculate what they will be. As an example, let's take an 11% fixed-rate loan with a remaining balance of $51,350. Imagine that the interest rate will be increased to 13% and the loan has 23 years to run. Using the amortization chart at the back of this book, look down the 13% column until you come to 23 years. The factor is 11.06. Multiply 11.06 by 51.350 (the number of thousands in the loan balance). The new monthly payment will be $567.93.

How Will You Finance The Rest?
If you have enough cash to pay the seller the difference between the loan balance and sales price, you won't need to read further. Most buyers are not in that position. There is often a hole in the transaction the size of the Grand Canyon, waiting to be bridged in the easiest way possible. An assumption is no bargain unless the secondary financing is also reasonably priced and the buyer is able to qualify (if necessary) for both the assumption and the secondary money.

In the previous section, we looked at Seller-financed Second Trust Deeds. They are an excellent and commonly-used financing method with an assumption. But what if the seller cannot or will not accept a note? One alternative is to find outside money, possibly a second mortgage from another source. With particularly good assumptions, wrap loans are another solution. These financing ideas will be covered in the following chapters.

ADVANTAGES OF AN ASSUMPTION
1. Lower closing costs and fees, as compared to new financing.
2. New buyer may take advantage of a lower-than-market interest rate on some assumptions.
3. Buyer may not have to qualify, although this is required on most of today's assumptions.

DISADVANTAGES OF AN ASSUMPTION
1. Excellent assumptions are hard to find.
2. There is a possibility that the Seller may not be released from liability.
3. If the interest rate increases, payments will be re-amortized over the remaining term.
4. Secondary financing is often necessary to bridge the gap.

CHAPTER 21

Purchase Money Seconds
Equity Seconds

PURCHASE MONEY SECOND

DEFINITION: **A Purchase Money Second Mortgage (or Trust Deed) loan is one which is obtained by a buyer for funds to purchase the property, in addition to a new or assumed first mortgage loan.**

A buyer needs a Purchase Money Second if the distance between the balance on the first mortgage and the sales price is more than the down payment can stretch.

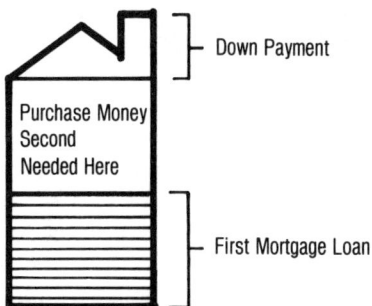

— Down Payment

Purchase Money
Second
Needed Here

— First Mortgage Loan

THE PURCHASE MONEY SECOND

I have already discussed one kind of Purchase Money Second: the seller-financed second trust deed loan, covered in an earlier chapter. That is often the best and least expensive way of financing the missing link. As an alternative, the buyer may obtain a second from a lending institution or private source other than the seller. This is the type we will deal with here.

Where To Get A Purchase Money Second

Private sources, such as parents or grandparents, are handy to have in situations like this. Presumably they like you and trust you, and so may be willing to offer far better terms than institutional lenders. The escrow officer who is handling the closing can prepare a note and trust deed or, if you prefer, ask an attorney to draw up the documents.

If you do not have a private source available to you, contact lending institutions such as banks, savings & loans, mortgage companies and mortgage brokers to find out if they offer seconds. Many institutions handle only first mortgage loans. To make the search easier, ask your real estate agent to direct you to the best prospects.

Interest Rates And Terms

Because a loan in second position is a greater risk to the lender than a first mortgage loan (as explained in the Seller Financing section), it will cost the borrower more. Interest rates on institutional seconds are at least $\frac{1}{2}$% to 2% higher than the rates on first mortgage loans. In addition, the term on a second is shorter, usually no more than 15 years.

Balloon Payments

Balloon payments (or calls) are frequently found on seconds. With a balloon, even though the payments are amortized over a longer period of time, (15 to 20 years, for example), the loan becomes due and payable at an earlier date (2 to 5 years from closing). Do not consider a second that has a balloon unless the amount of the second is small and you are sure you will have funds on hand to pay it off. Never count on refinancing the loan to pay the balloon. You risk losing your home if you are not able to come up with the necessary cash. Instead, choose a loan that is fully amortized, with no balloon.

Fixed Or Adjustable Rates

Seconds may have either fixed or adjustable interest rates. Before making a decision, study the chapters in this book that cover both types of conventional financing and discuss the pros and cons of each with the loan officer. Interest rate and monthly payments may be lower at first with an adjustable rate second but could end up considerably higher.

Loan-To-Value Ratio
The loan-to-value ratio on seconds is usually much lower than on first mortgages. While first mortgage loans may go as high as 95% LTV, lenders commonly set maximums of 70% to 80% LTV for seconds. That means that the total of the first and second loan amounts may not exceed 70% (or 80%) of the appraised value of the home.

Note that private lenders (parents, relatives etc.) are not bound by these limits. They should, however, check with an accountant or the IRS to learn the tax regulations which apply to this type of financing. Since the lender in this case is not the seller, the imputed interest rule mentioned in the chapter on Contracts does not apply, but other rules do.

Qualifying For A Second
Lending institutions use the same standards to qualify buyers for seconds as for first mortgage loans. However, the monthly payments for both loans are added together and the total is used in the calculations. For example, if a buyer is planning to assume a loan with monthly payments of $525, and is applying for a second with payments of $175, then the sum of the two, $700, will be used for qualifying. Instructions are given in a later chapter, Qualifying For A Loan.

Seconds With A New First Mortgage Loan
While seconds are most often used with assumptions, there are situations where the buyer obtains both a new first mortgage loan and a second from different sources. For instance, DVA home loans have a maximum limit of $63,000. If the buyer needs more than that amount, he or she may obtain a second mortgage from either the seller or another source. Loan-to-value ratios for both DVA and the second lender must be followed, and the buyer must be able to qualify for the sum of both payments.

When A Purchase Money Second Doesn't Make Sense
Unless the first mortgage loan has a particularly low interest rate, or unless the second mortgage is a temporary measure for a very short period of time, this method of financing may not be practical. Second mortgage money from an institutional lender is expensive, and that higher rate could cancel the advantage from an average assumption. This is especially true if the second is for a large amount.

Another drawback is that monthly payments on an institutional second are higher than for a first mortgage loan, because of the shorter term and the higher rate. This, therefore, affects a buyer's ability to qualify. Unless the payments on the assumed loan are unusually low, a buyer may find it easier to qualify for a new first mortgage loan than for an assumption plus institutional second.

A buyer with a small down payment will be foiled by the 70% loan-to-value ratio on an institutional second, but could borrow up to 95% of the appraised value on a conventional first mortgage loan (and even higher on some government loans). For this, as in any other type of financing, use your common sense to determine what would be best for you.

ADVANTAGE OF A PURCHASE MONEY SECOND
1. Allows the buyer to take advantage of a low interest rate on the first mortgage loan, while still providing the necessary cash to purchase the property.

DISADVANTAGES OF A PURCHASE MONEY SECOND
1. Interest rate is higher than for a first mortgage loan.
2. Term of the loan is shorter.
3. Because of these, payments are higher, possibly making it more difficult to qualify for financing.
4. Loan-to-value ratio is low, requiring a larger down payment.

EQUITY SECOND

DEFINITION: **An Equity Second Mortgage (or Trust Deed) loan is one which is obtained by the owner, as a cash payment for part of his or her equity.**

There is a very subtle difference between a Purchase Money Second and an Equity Second. With the exception of the borrower's signature on the bottom line and reason for obtaining the loan, they are essentially the same. Purchase money seconds are obtained by the buyer of a home at the time of purchase, while equity seconds are borrowed by the person who already owns the property.

Owners choose second mortgage loans for one of two reasons. First, they are a useful refinancing tool. Equity seconds provide an opportunity to cash in part of the equity that has been building over the years, without losing the advantage of a low interest rate on the underlying loan.

Case History: Harry and Rose Miller
Harry and Rose went to their youngest son's college graduation ceremony, and flew to Europe that evening for a vacation. The last tuition payment and the entire European spree was paid for by means of an equity second. As Rose explained, "We've been pouring money into our home for fourteen years and had almost $60,000 in equity. Yet after putting three sons through college, we didn't have enough money in savings to pay for the trip we had promised ourselves."

The Millers considered refinancing their home so that they could use some of that equity. But their existing loan was at 5%. That would be hard to give up! Current rates were around 13% for a new fixed rate loan. With the help of a loan officer, the Millers calculated loan costs, monthly payments and income tax advantages, and finally decided to apply for a second mortgage at 14.25%. Their monthly payments have increased but the extra interest also brings an additional tax advantage.

Equity Second As A Buying And Selling Tool
Another use of the equity second is to help buy or sell a home. If you have watched one of the late-night TV seminars, designed to make you a real-estate millionaire with no money down, you have heard of this technique. According to the proponents, a buyer (presumably one who is unable to get financing) asks the seller to obtain an equity second for the amount of cash the seller needs at closing. The buyer then assumes the first and second mortgage loans, or buys the home on contract. The no-money-down advisor usually goes a step further: the seller is asked to carry a note for the balance of the sales price, secured by a third deed of trust.

Sounds simple! The seller receives cash at closing and is able to sell the home. The buyer, with a poor credit rating and no cash, is able to buy. But the real world of real estate finance is not always that uncomplicated. Here are the problems: first, not all seconds are assumable. Those lenders that allow their seconds to be assumed pay close attention to the new buyer's credit worthiness. Because second position carries a higher risk for the lender, most are understandably fussy about who buys the home on contract.

Sellers should be extremely cautious: this could be dangerous financing to consider. If you, the seller, obtain an equity second for the sole purpose of selling your home, make sure beforehand that the loan is assumable or that you will have the right to sell on contract. Find out if the buyer must qualify to assume the loan and then determine if your prospective buyer will pass the test. If the sale cannot take place, you may be left with an expensive loan. It is far safer, instead, to have the buyer finance the home, with the seller's help (if necessary) in paying the loan costs.

ADVANTAGES OF AN EQUITY SECOND
1. The owner receives cash for part of the equity.
2. The first mortgage loan (with possibly a low interest rate) remains intact.

DISADVANTAGES OF AN EQUITY SECOND
1. Interest rate and payments may be higher than for a new first mortgage loan.
2. Risky for a seller to use as a sales tool.

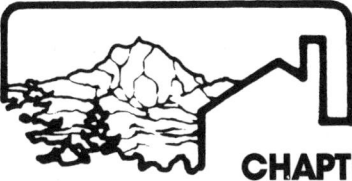

CHAPTER 22
Wrap Loans

DEFINITION: **A Wrap Loan is a mortgage loan that is "wrapped" around an existing loan. The lender assumes the existing first mortgage loan and supplies additional funds.**

A Wrap Loan is similar at first glance to a land sales contract, but with an outside lender providing financing rather than the seller. Here is how the two compare:

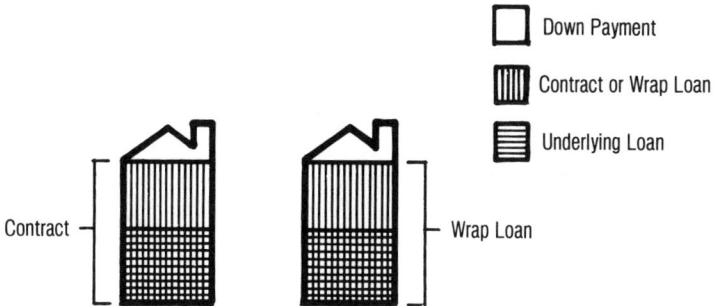

COMPARING THE WRAP LOAN AND CONTRACT

The one essential ingredient in wrap loan financing is an underlying loan. (That, of course, is not true of a contract, which may be used with or without existing financing.) In addition, the underlying loan must be assumable. With a wrap, the lender assumes the existing loan, adds additional funds as needed and offers a new loan to the borrower at an interest rate that blends the rate of the underlying loan with the rate charged for the new funds.

Where To Obtain A Wrap Loan

Some conventional lending institutions (banks, S&Ls, mortgage companies etc.) provide wrap financing, although many do not. Some lenders offer it only when they have financed the existing loan; others will wrap any assumable loan, no matter what its source. A few lenders will even wrap an assumable contract, if it is written to their specifications. Your real estate agent can help you find an institution that offers the kind of wrap loans you need.

Calculating The Interest Rate

Since a wrap loan is a blend of new and old funds, the resulting interest rate is also a blend of the two. Lenders use a special yield chart that takes into account the ratio of new money to old, the interest rate on the existing loan, and the yield required by the lender. Ask a loan officer to calculate the blended rate for your particular situation.

Many assumable loans are not worth wrapping. In general, the lower the percentage of new money required, the lower the rate on the underlying loan and the newer the existing loan, the more favorable the blended rate and monthly payments will be. A wrap loan has a term that equals the term on the assumed loan. If, for instance, the underlying loan has 23 years left, the new wrap loan will also have a 23-year term. Payments will be amortized over 23 years, making them higher than payments on a 30-year loan at the same rate.

Wrap Loan vs Second Mortgage Loan

One advantage a wrap loan has over a purchase money second is the loan-to-value ratio. Because the lender has control over the underlying mortgage in wrap financing, the risk is reduced. Many lenders will loan as high as 95% LTV for a wrap, yet only 70% or 80% LTV on a second mortgage. In plain English, this means that buyers with low down payments can often obtain a wrap loan, but not a second.

Case History: Robin Masters

Robin put in an offer to buy a home that had a wonderfully assumable loan. The $51,000 loan balance could be assumed at 8%. Robin offered a price of $86,000, with a down payment of $4300 (5% of the purchase price). She needed to finance the $30,700 difference.

We checked on the possibility of a wrap loan. The loan officer consulted the chart, ran a few quick calculations, and came up with a blended rate of 11.25% for a new $81,700 wrap loan. Compared to the current rate of 12.75% (for a 30-year fixed rate loan), the blended rate was a bargain.

The payments, however, were not as low as Robin had hoped. Since the original 30-year loan was 9 years old, the wrap loan had only 21 years to run. That meant monthly principal and interest payments of $846.41. A new fixed rate loan at the higher rate would have payments of $888, surprisingly close.

An institutional second mortgage was out of the question here, since Robin needed a 95% LTV. Her down payment was only 5%, far less than a lender would require for a second.

Other financing methods, such as an ARM or a GPARM, would have given Robin lower payments initially, with no greater closing costs, but the wrap loan gave her the assurance of 21 years of fixed payments.

Considering that few assumptions are as attractive as the one Robin found, it is not surprising that wrap loans are not widely used. It takes just the right set of circumstances to produce a blended rate and monthly payments that are attractively lower than those on a new loan.

ADVANTAGES OF A WRAP LOAN

1. Lower interest rate than on a standard new loan.
2. Higher loan-to-value ratios than on a second mortgage.

DISADVANTAGES OF A WRAP LOAN

1. Payments amortized over a shorter term, therefore they are greater than for a 30-year loan at the same rate.
2. Very few assumption situations produce outstanding wrap loans.

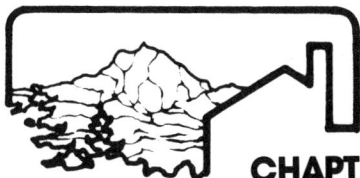

CHAPTER 23

Selling A Note

DEFINITION: **Seller-financed contracts and notes may be sold at a discounted price, in order to provide cash for the seller.**

There never seems to be enough cash to go around. That is particularly true of real estate transactions involving seller-financing. An offer may be perfect in every other respect: top sales price, qualified buyers, agreeable contract terms, and ideal closing date. But if it does not give the seller the cash he or she needs, it will probably be rejected.

The cash problem is a thorny one. Where can you find additional cash, if both buyer and seller have reached their limits? In this book, I have talked about dozens of ways to finance a home, most of which involve new loans. However there may be reasons why a buyer does not choose new financing. The underlying loan may be assumable at an enticingly low rate, or the home may need some major repairs before it can be financed. In each case, selling a seller-financed note or contract may be just the answer.

How To Sell A Note Or Contract

There are companies and individuals who buy contracts and secured notes (notes secured by a trust deed or mortgage) for cash. There is a hitch: selling a note or contract can be expensive. Instead of paying the face value (the actual amount financed), the note or contract is discounted and the seller receives the lower (discounted) amount.

What Investors Look For In A Note

How much the face value will be discounted depends upon many factors, such as the lien position (first, second or third), interest rate, amount of the monthly payment and term, to name a few. Investors (buyers of the notes) use a yield chart to determine what discount to charge, so that their income from the note will yield the desired return on their investment.

Not all investors think alike. Some refuse to buy a note or contract with a balloon payment because of the risk of default. Others think positively with respect to balloons; they consider the early payoff an asset. Some investors want only seasoned notes, those that have been in effect for a few years. Others will buy new notes as readily as old. Many investors specialize in one type of document. For instance, they may buy only trust deed notes and not contracts, or only notes of a specific size.

As a general guideline, the higher the monthly payment and the shorter the term of the note or contract, the higher the price it will bring. Investors like to see hefty payments, amortized over as short a term as possible.

How Much Will Be Discounted?
This is the part that makes sellers nervous. Their first reaction is often a violent one, as they convince themselves that this crazy scheme will never work. Have patience. If the discount cost I am about to mention seems high to you, read on. There are ways to minimize the loss.

You can expect the average second trust deed note or contract to be discounted approximately 20% to 35%. In other words, a seller can expect to receive 65% to 80% of the face value of the second or in the case of a contract, the equity value. But just as each investor looks for different features in a note or contract, so do the discounted prices vary from one investor to another. Recently I gave a sample note to five investors and received five widely differing prices, all within the range mentioned above.

It is possible to sell for higher than 80% of the face value, if the note or contract includes terms that are particularly endearing to the investor. For this reason, it is a good idea to talk to investors before agreeing to carry a note or contract that you expect to sell at closing or at a later time. Learn what features will make the note more saleable and bring you a higher price.

Here is a situation where buyers and sellers cooperated to make a transaction work:

Case History: The Moores and The Parkers

Julie and Tom Moore wanted to buy the Parkers' home. Jean and Sam Parker needed every penny they could muster for the down payment on their new home, and so they insisted on a cash-out transaction.

"No way!" said the buyers. "We're attracted to your assumable loan as well as your greenhouse and hot tub. We are willing to pay your asking price if you will please carry a note for the $8,000 difference."

The Parkers objected violently. By the time they paid all their closing costs, there would be very little left out of the down payment. They needed more cash. Offer rejected!

Fortunately they had a real estate agent who wouldn't give up that easily. She suggested that they investigate the possibility of selling a note. The Parkers would agree to carry a note secured by a second deed of trust and would sell that note at closing to an investor. They showed the Moores' offer to several investors, to determine what price they could expect. When Sam Parker heard the results, prices of $4,000 to $5,000 for the $8,000 note, he decided not to move.

"But wait," begged the persistent agent. "Let's try changing the terms of the note, to see if we can improve the price." The agent asked the investors what terms would make them happiest. "Higher interest rate," said one. "Shorter term," said another. Larger payments were important to all.

The trick was to find a combination of all these factors that would bring the best possible price. The resulting note combined an interest rate of 13.5% (up from the original 11%) and payments that increased each month for the first twelve months, on the same principal as a GEM loan. With these increased payments, the $8,000 note would be paid in full (without a balloon) in just under three years. It brought the Parkers, at closing, a price of $6,750, just $1,250 less than face value.

The Parkers were lucky that the buyers were willing and able to cooperate in order to make this work. Not only were the Moores willing to pay the higher interest rate and payments, but they were also able to meet the additional requirements of the investor: it was necessary for them to qualify for the combined payments on both loans and to have a down payment at least 10% of the value of the home. Because the first mortgage loan could be assumed at an excellent rate, Julie and Tom Moore were delighted with their financing package. And the Parkers? Who wouldn't be thrilled to come that close to an all-cash full-price transaction?

Sell Only What You Need
Another technique to reduce the size of the discount could be nicknamed the Sell-A-Note/Keep-A-Note idea. This is designed for the seller who does not need to receive cash for the entire amount of the equity. Let's imagine that a seller is asked to carry a $30,000 note, secured by a second trust deed. If the seller were to sell that note, it might bring only $19,000 to $24,000. That means a loss of from $6,000 to $11,000.

But let's suppose that the seller does not actually need that much cash. $10,000 would do nicely, thank you. Instead of selling one large $30,000 note, the seller could divide that equity into two notes, a $13,000 and a $17,000 note, for example, each secured by a separate trust deed. By selling the $13,000 note, the seller could collect the desired $10,000 while losing only $3,000 to discounting. He or she could carry the remaining note, collecting principal and interest each month from the buyer.

In this technique the position of the notes is important. If there is also an underlying loan, one of the notes will be in second position, the other will be a third trust deed note. As explained in the chapter "Seller-Financed Second Deed Of Trust", a third trust deed note is less desirable and potentially more of a risk than a second. Therefore a third trust deed note would bring a considerably lower price than the range I quoted above. In fact, many investors refuse to buy any note beyond a second. For these reasons, a seller usually sells the second trust deed note and carries the third. Keep in mind, though, in the case of foreclosure, the holder of the third will be third in line for reimbursement.

Not Every Note Is Saleable
As the Moores and Parkers discovered, investors do not buy every note that is offered. They have specific requirements in addition to the terms of the note. Buyers whose credit is poor or who have insufficient income to qualify for all monthly payments will find it difficult to enter into this type of financing. Most investors require a credit report, to be paid for by the buyer.

Many investors require a down payment of at least 10% of the home's value; some insist on 20% or 25% down. How that value is determined is up to the individual investor. Many, but not all, want a professional appraisal, paid for by the buyer or seller. This amount is often deducted from the discount fee at closing. Homes that do not pass an institutional lender's rigid scrutiny may still be acceptable to some investors. Standards vary; if the condition of the property is less than perfect, look for an investor willing to overlook the defects.

Where To Find Investors
Although there are dozens of ads in daily newspapers, offering to buy notes and contracts, the easiest way to find a reputable investor is through word-of-mouth. Real estate agents can often suggest the names of local companies specializing in small note purchases.

ADVANTAGES OF SELLING
A NOTE OR CONTRACT

1. Seller receives cash at time of sale.
2. Cheaper for the buyer than a new loan.
3. Some investors will consider less-than-perfect property.

DISADVANTAGES OF SELLING
A NOTE OR CONTRACT

1. The discount can be costly, an expense usually absorbed by the seller.
2. Buyers must be qualified for total payments.

CHAPTER 24

Sweat Equity

DEFINITION: **Sweat Equity is equity that is created through improvements made to the property by the purchaser. The value of these improvements may be considered part of the buyer's down payment.**

It sounds very simple. Take one "fixer-upper", a home that needs substantial repair in order to qualify for financing. Add a buyer who is willing and able to tackle the job. The result: an ideal situation for sweat equity.

There are plenty of homes on the market that are in too poor a condition to be financed. Institutional and government lenders are very particular about the properties in which they invest. It would be utter foolishness to issue a 30-year loan for a home that will be sagging at the seams in five years.

That leaves many sellers in a difficult spot. They could, of course, make the necessary repairs, but only if they have the time, skill or money. The less-than-perfect home may be sold on contract, but that would not offer the cash many sellers need. And selling a contract to generate cash is not always easy when the property is in need of repair.

There is another alternative. The buyers may be willing to pay for or make the necessary repairs, in order to obtain a new loan. The value of the repair work may be credited to the buyers at closing, as all or part of their down payment. If the work is actually done by the buyers themselves, this amount is known as sweat equity.

Sweat Equity Problems

Since problems cling to sweat equity cases like burrs to a dog, most lenders groan at the mere mention of the words. The difficulties lie in determining what work is to be done, who is to provide the materials and what the value of the sweat equity will be. It may sound straightforward and foolproof at the outset, but as soon as the buyer uncovers some unexpected structural damage or a bad case of hidden dryrot, the fireworks begin.

The last time I worked on a sweat equity transaction for a client, both buyers and sellers came close to apoplexy and a legal battle. Repairs proved to be far more costly than originally planned and neither buyers nor sellers had the cash necessary to continue. Fortunately it had a happy ending, thanks to a supplier who provided materials on credit. But for a long time afterward, I vowed never to get involved in a sweat equity arrangement again.

Lending Guidelines For Sweat Equity

Lenders feel exactly the same apprehension. Many institutions refuse to allow sweat equity. Those that do have established certain rules to help control the situation. Each lending institution has different guidelines, so be sure to discuss your lender's particular policies with the loan officer. Here are some general rules that many lenders follow.

Work That Will "Count" As Sweat Equity

A buyer may want to put in a brand new kitchen, complete with tile counters, a greenhouse window and lighted ceiling. Total cost: $2,000 in materials, $4,000 worth of labor by the buyer. The seller says "Fine with me! That $6,000 can be the down payment for your new loan."

Lending institutions may not agree. They usually allow as sweat equity only those repairs deemed necessary for financing. The buyer in the example above might finish the kitchen, with the seller's blessing, then find that the lender will not allow it to "count" as part of the down payment. The buyer could be forced to come up with a cash down payment. If this is not possible, he or she may not be able to get financing. The seller would have a much-improved home and the poor buyer could lose the time and money invested.

To avoid this problem, most lenders insist that loan application be made and an appraisal be ordered by the loan officer (paid for by either the buyer or seller) before any work has begun. The appraiser will determine exactly what needs to be done in order to obtain financing and it is this list of repairs only that will "count" as sweat equity. After the loan has been approved by the lender, subject to the repairs being made, of course, it is safe for the buyer to start work on the property.

Determining The Value Of The Sweat Equity
A buyer may feel that his or her labor is worth a certain figure, but most lenders want proof. Many require three estimates of labor and materials from professional builders or remodelers to establish a fair value for the sweat equity. Some include the cost of materials and labor, others will allow the buyer to count only the value of the labor alone.

Lending institutions are always hesitant to let a buyer use sweat equity for the total amount of the down payment. They would prefer to see at least 5% of the appraised value in cash, with the sweat equity increasing the down payment by an additional 5% or 10%. Some lenders will, with caution, accept sweat equity instead of cash for the entire down payment. If this is what you need, call different lending institutions until you find one that will accommodate you.

FHA has an additional requirement. Although FHA will consider sweat equity instead of a cash down payment, FHA borrowers must show evidence that they have the necessary skill and time to complete the job in a professional manner.

The Agreement Between Buyer And Seller
Disagreement over money matters is the major source of sweat equity problems. Buyers and sellers who enter into a sweat equity transaction should have a written
167

agreement (included as part of the sales agreement) that specifies exactly who will pay for what. While it is hard to plan for all the unforeseen difficulties that could occur, the agreement should cover the worst possible scenario. Who will cover the cost of additional repairs that are found to be necessary while the work is in progress? Who will do the extra work? How will this affect the sales price and down payment amount already agreed upon? Buyers and sellers should consider asking for legal advice from their attorneys in order to avoid a bitter disagreement later.

Final Evaluation
When the work has been completed, the loan officer will ask the appraiser to re-inspect the property. The fee for this inspection is usually $25 to $50 dollars, but varies from lender to lender. If the repairs are satisfactory, the closing may take place. If more work is required, another re-inspection and fee will be necessary.

ADVANTAGES OF SWEAT EQUITY
1. Buyer may turn elbow grease into down payment money.
2. Seller receives cash for the equity.
3. A problem property is sold.

DISADVANTAGES OF SWEAT EQUITY
1. Lenders are cautious; not every one will allow sweat equity. Rules are rigid.
2. Disagreements and unforeseen problems can be disastrous.

CHAPTER 25

Buying With No Money Down

Late-night television has become the stomping ground for the no-money-down gurus. "You, too," they croon, "can go out tomorrow and, in just five short hours, buy a piece of property with not one cent for down payment." Can it really be done? And more importantly, can it be done without investing in the high-cost instruction materials offered through these television seminars?

The answer to both questions is yes. Buying a home with no money down is entirely possible. In this chapter, we'll discuss some of the basic techiques for accomplishing this. On your own or with the help of a competent real estate agent, you would be able to enter into an agreement to buy a home without spending a dollar. But before you leap at the opportunity, consider the cautionary note sounded here. Sometimes a no-money-down transaction will be more of a liability than an asset. Read this chapter carefully, then decide whether or not you want to proceed.

If You Are A Veteran . . .
First let's clear the slate by looking at two special-interest groups that may buy with no money down: veterans and low-income borrowers.

If you are a veteran who is qualified for a federal VA loan, you are in a fortunate position. 100% LTV financing is available for most homes under $110,000. By asking the seller to pay your closing costs, you can buy a home with no cash outlay. True, you must find a seller who is willing to foot the bill for the extra costs plus the required discount points and seller's closing costs, but many are willing to do so, in order to receive cash at closing for the remaining equity.

If You Are A Low-Income Borrower . . .

Farmers Home Administration loans are also available up to 100% LTV, for low-income borrowers who want to buy a modest home in a designated rural area. Refer back to the FmHA chapter for more information about this type of financing.

Other 100% LTV Financing

The rest of the population will not have 100% LTV financing offered on a silver platter. Lending institutions and other government lenders require some cash as down payment. Sellers who are willing to carry a contract or second have no such limitations, although they may find it necessary or prudent to ask for a cash investment from the borrower. If you are a prospective buyer, without sufficient cash to satisfy the conventional lenders, your best chance (other than the two loans mentioned above) of financing a home is through a land sales contract or simple assumption plus seller-financed second.

When you put in an offer to buy a property with no down payment, you will run into an immediate problem: almost everyone loves the sound of cold, hard cash. Most sellers would prefer to wait until hell freezes over, rather than transfer the property to a buyer with no down payment. Overcoming an owner's objections will be your greatest hurdle. There are certain inescapable closing costs for any transaction (see chapter on Loan Fees And Closing Costs) and you will have to find a seller who is willing and able to pay them. Here are some promising signs to look for when you are house-hunting:

* property that has been on the market for a long time
* a vacant home
* surplus property (an investment property, an extra home as the result of a marriage, etc.)
* a home with an obvious, but repairable flaw, such as peeling paint
* advertisements that use the words "owner desperate", "must sell", or "anxious"

* advertisements promising that the owner will pay all the closing costs
* property with no existing loan, or one that will permit a contract sale or owner-financed second with no strings attached.

A seller who has no other prospective buyers in sight and who can afford to sell with no money down may accept a reasonable offer. A top sales price and a high interest rate on the offer should produce even better results. Sellers who have other alternatives, however, may be hesitant and may need to be convinced that this offer is a financial benefit. You or your real estate agent can pull together figures to illustrate the advantages. Stress, for example, that this offer will bring:

* an excellent interest return on the seller's equity
* a steady income over the term of the contract or second
* an immediate sale
* immediate relief from tax, insurance and existing loan payments
* immediate relief from maintenance and repair expense.

Try to mold your offer to the seller's needs. The one thing you cannot provide is cash at closing, but other points may also be important, such as the overall sales price, the closing date, the interest rate, the size of the monthly payments, the term of the contract, and even your willingness to let the seller have all the draperies or the rose bushes. By agreeing with the seller in some areas, you may win the issue that is most important to you, a no-money-down transaction.

Here are some techniques that are sometimes used to make a no-down-payment offer more attractive to a hesitant seller:

Lump-Sum Payments
You do not have cash for the seller at closing, but could you build a down payment over the early years of the loan? Additional lump-sum payments ($250, $1,000, or whatever you can afford) can be made at pre-arranged

intervals (every 3 months, 6 months, year, etc.). This would give the seller extra cash and would build up your equity.

Sweat Equity
Although sweat equity was discussed in an earlier chapter, it deserves to be mentioned in a no-money-down context. Institutional lenders are reluctant to accept sweat equity in place of the entire down payment; most require at least a small cash contribution. But sellers are under no such constraint. Sweat equity can work beautifully here for two reasons: first, a home is sold that might otherwise linger on the market, and second, the value of the home is increased after the repairs have been made. This will give the seller an opportunity to sell the note, or you, the buyer may now have sufficient equity to refinance the home.

Shared Appreciation
Shared appreciation is a technique favored by many of the television seminar instructors. In Oregon, however, the idea fizzled during the early 80s, since there was very little appreciation to share in the housing market. Here is how it works: for a no-money-down transaction, the seller agrees to forego a cash down payment, in exchange for a share of the appreciation (profit) when the home is sold or refinanced on a certain, agreed-upon date. In other words, if a home with a purchase price of $50,000 in 1985 is worth $62,000 four years later, the seller would be entitled to a percentage of that $12,000. Obviously this technique is no asset to a seller when market values are dropping, but there are side benefits which can be attractive. This will be discussed in the section on Equity Participation below.

Because of the complexity of a shared appreciation transaction, an attorney should prepare the necessary documents.

Refinance With Assumption
Even though this is often mentioned as a no-money-down technique, I have found that it is not easy to accomplish. Here the seller refinances the home before the sale, allowing the buyer to assume the loan at closing. This could be done with a first- or second-

mortgage loan. Problems occur at the time of the assumption: lenders often refuse to let a buyer with no cash investment assume the loan. To solve this difficulty, the following technique was invented.

Equity Participation (Equity Sharing)
IRS will permit only those persons who hold title to a piece of property to claim the tax benefits derived from that parcel. There are times when a seller would find it advantageous to share those benefits, in exchange for accepting a no-cash offer. (Note: current proposed tax changes may reduce the desirability of this technique. Consult a tax accountant before trying it.)

The owner of a piece of property may, instead of actually selling the home, remain in title with the new buyer. The two would jointly refinance the property using the original owner's equity. This does not mean that both parties must live in the home. One may be an occupant-borrower, the other a non-occupant borrower (usually the original owner) or, in the case of investment property, both may be non-occupant borrowers.

The advantage to the new owner is that this is a no-money-down transaction (some closing costs may even be financed). He or she must qualify for only a portion of the loan since the other owner will qualify for the remaining percentage. To the original owner's benefit is the tax advantage of property ownership (subject to change) and the possibility of receiving cash for some of the equity at the time of refinance. Since many lenders will loan only up to 85% LTV on a refinance, equity participation works best when the original owner had substantial equity.

This technique is often used in another way. The non-occupant borrower may be a person other than the owner of the property. In exchange for a cash investment and qualifying for a portion of a new loan, he or she will receive tax benefits and a share of future appreciation. In this way, equity participation and shared appreciation go hand-in-hand.

Equity participation involves an agreement between the two parties, as well as the joint finance agreement

173

with the lender. As such, it is a complicated technique that should be used only with competent legal and tax advice.

Why A No-Money-Down Transaction May Not Be Desirable

Most sellers would rather avoid "all this funny business". They want a straightforward sale with plenty of cash. Therefore, the buyer or the real estate agent may have a tough selling job, convincing the owner that the offer is an attractive one, albeit unusual.

If the home is in good condition and is well-priced, a no-money-down offer is at a disadvantage. The best properties will be sold via cash, new loans, or seller financing that includes a down payment. Buyers without cash for a down payment will have a very limited choice on the housing market and will often have to pay top price for the privilege of a no-money-down transaction. With the exception of VA and FmHA buyers, the no-money-downers will usually be left with the dregs, those properties that have serious problems or have not been sold after months on the market. While there are exceptions, this is generally the case.

There is another factor to keep in mind: a 100% LTV loan has higher monthly payments than, for instance, a 90% or 95% LTV loan at the same interest rate. For 30-year financing at 12% interest, on a home worth $65,000, the amortized monthly payments would be approximately $669 for a 100% LTV loan, $635 with a 5% down payment and $602 with 10% down. The difference in payment amount can push a buyer out of the financial comfort zone.

If you are a prospective buyer, consider whether or not you want to buy under these conditions. It is often a better idea to wait until you have saved a small down payment; your range of choice will improve dramatically and your monthly payments will be lower. Once you have a down payment, many a seller will be willing to pay your buyer's closing costs in order to be cashed out by a new loan. No-money-down is certainly possible but the results may not be as desirable as the television seminars would lead us to believe.

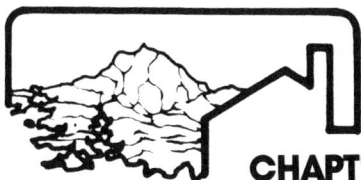

CHAPTER 26

Special Situations:

Refinancing A Home
New Construction Financing
Financing A Mobile Home

REFINANCING A HOME

There are many reasons for refinancing a home. Some owners can find a better use for the cash that is currently tied up as equity. Others are tired of paying higher interest rates than those currently available. Many owners have a balloon payment due on a contract, and must refinance or sell. Still others want to change the type of loan, from an ARM, for instance, to fixed-rate financing.

Approach the idea of refinancing with caution. Like any new loan, a refinance is expensive. The lending institution that provided the first mortgage loan may offer a slightly reduced loan fee for certain refinances. An exception to this is the replacement of a high-interest loan with a new one at a lower rate; do not expect a concession in this case.

Usually the same closing costs associated with any new loan will be charged for a refinance. Studies have indicated that, because of this expense, it is unwise to refinance a high-interest loan for one with less than a 2% difference in interest. Calculate the costs versus the savings of the new loan with the help of a loan officer. Be aware, too, of other aspects of the exchange. For example, many older loans had better assumption privileges than new loans. Don't trade your home's future saleability for questionable benefits.

Second Trust Deed Loan As An Alternative
If your goal is to obtain cash for your equity, give serious thought to a second mortgage or trust deed loan. This is especially true if your interest rate is attractively low by today's standards. Depending upon the rates of the existing and new loans, a second may be a less expensive alternative to a whole new first mortgage loan.

Avoid Refinancing by Pre-Planning
Whenever you buy a home, plan ahead. If at all possible, choose permanent financing that will not need to be replaced. Sometimes, though, a refinance is unavoidable. If so, take the time to shop around for the best loan possible. By all means contact the lender who holds the underlying mortgage but don't stop there. Get a second opinion, then several more, before making your decision.

FINANCING NEW CONSTRUCTION

Financing a home to be built is not quite as easy as financing an existing one. New construction is riskier for lenders; most are unwilling to enter into a 30-year commitment based upon a set of plans and the gleam in a prospective owner's eye.

The problem is this: until the construction is complete, the home is not much of an asset. In the case of a default by the borrower, the lender may be left with nothing but a half-finished basement. Additional concerns about the quality of construction compound the risk. Lenders have only the builder's word that the home will be built in an acceptable manner.

Over the years, a system of safeguards has been adopted to avoid such problems. First, temporary financing, known as the Construction Loan, must be secured to pay for the costs of building the home. Once construction is complete, a permanent loan may be obtained. This can mean added cost for the borrower, with two loan closings and a double set of fees. Some lenders today are offering a special "package deal": both the construction loan and permanent financing are included in one loan, with one closing and one set of fees. (The loan fee for this service is often a substantial one and it may not actually save the borrower money when compared to the two-step method.) Some institutions will agree to "lock" in the interest rate on the permanent financing as of the date of the initial loan approval, for a certain number of days. This prevents a problem many buyers have encountered. By the time construction is finished, interest rates may be so high that they can no longer qualify for permanent financing and so lose the home through foreclosure.

How A Construction Loan Works

Construction funds may be borrowed by either the builder or the buyer. Most lenders feel that it is easier to loan the money directly to the builder. If the buyer secures the construction loan, the builder usually must also be approved by the lender. Some institutions will finance only projects built by specific, tried-and-true contractors. Others will work with any builder who can supply adequate credentials and a satisfactory financial picture. It is difficult for a buyer who wants to act as builder to obtain a construction loan, unless he or she has had previous experience.

Funds for building the home are not dispersed at closing, but are released in a series of draws, at various stages of construction. Lenders often ask for proof that subcontractors and suppliers have been paid by the builder, before releasing additional money. Construction liens filed against the property by unpaid claimants can lead directly to foreclosure, or at the very least to considerable expense for the owner and lender. When construction has been complete, a lender will insist upon waiting for the lien period to lapse before issuing the permanent financing. Buyers who do not wish to wait 60 days will usually be required to pay for an "Early Issue" endorsement on the mortgagee's title insurance policy, to protect the lender against unforeseen liens. This costs from $1.50 to $2.50 per $1,000 of loan amount and is usually available only when the builder is qualified and approved by the title insurance company.

In addition, a foundation survey is required for most new construction, to assure the lender that the home to be financed conforms with the designated setback and building lines. This will cost the borrower $45 to $75. Other loan fees and closing costs are the same for new and existing homes.

New Construction With Government Financing
FHA and VA loans are available for new homes that meet their specifications, but neither will insure nor guarantee construction loans. Both will, however, issue a commitment for permanent financing before construction begins, so that the buyer, lender and builder know that the loan will be available. Many FHA/VA lenders also offer conventional construction loans and can handle both temporary and permanent financing.

For new homes that have already been built, but are less than 18 months old, FHA and VA loans are readily available for those built by FHA-, VA-, or HOW-approved contractors. Homes by non-approved contractors may also be financed under certain circumstances.

As mentioned in the chapter dealing with the Oregon Department of Veterans' Affairs, DVA may release funds during construction to a registered contractor who buys a performance bond. The cost of the bond is expensive, however, and most contractors prefer to use temporary financing from another source. (Note that even though DVA loans are not available for refinances, temporary construction loans are permitted.)

While the Oregon Single Family Mortgage Purchase Program officially covers new construction, few, if any, participating lenders are willing to handle such loans at this time.

FmHA offers permanent financing for a new home but a temporary construction loan must be obtained from another source. The builder must be one approved by FmHA.

FINANCING A MOBILE HOME

Mobile homes listed on the county tax rolls as real property, in other words, those permanently placed on property owned by the borrower, are financed with the type of loans discussed in this book. The homes must have permanent foundations with secure anchors, according to the lender's specifications. They are appraised before loan approval, just as site-built homes are evaluated. The one significant difference in financing a mobile home is the term of the loan. Many lenders are reluctant to extend full 30-year loans; often a 25-year term is the maximum available. The appraiser determines the life expectancy for the mobile home and the term of the loan will not exceed this figure.

Mobile homes on rented lots or without permanent foundations are treated as personal property. Loans are not offered by the mortgage loan department of the lending institution but are handled in much the same way an automobile is financed. Many lenders prefer to finance new homes exclusively; others provide loans for older mobiles as well. Terms are usually shorter than those for real property. For these homes, a maximum term of 15 years is customary, but this may be reduced for homes with a shorter life expectancy. Banks, S&Ls, finance companies and credit unions are good sources for loans and many of these work directly through mobile home dealers to finance new units.

Part VI
Securing A Loan

CHAPTER 27
Qualifying For A Loan

If you've been toying with the idea of buying the lumber baron's mansion on the hill overlooking town, study this chapter before you fall irrevocably in love with the place. It's a good idea to know where you stand in the matter of financing, in order to eliminate the risk of a broken heart.

Just how large a loan can you expect to get from a lender, considering your particular income and debts? Is the lumber baron's mansion within your financing capabilities, or should you be shopping for a three-bedroom ranch? To find the answers to these questions, "qualify" yourself, using the instructions that follow. Or ask a loan officer or real estate agent to do the calculations for you. (Please note that real estate agents and many loan officers work on a commission basis rather than on a salary. In return, they would like to have an opportunity to do business with you when you are ready to buy, sell or borrow.)

The methods used to qualify borrowers vary with different types of loans. While there is some standardization among conventional lenders, governmental agencies each have their own special computation techniques. The important thing for a prospective borrower to do first, however, is to get a general idea of his or her financial comfort zone. That is the purpose of the Ballpark Estimate below. By following the instructions, you will have a rough idea of the size of loan you could receive. Although the directions are based on conventional qualifying methods, the results will be reasonably close to government loan standards to give an approximate amount there, too. That will help you decide whether to inspect the lumber baron's mansion or to cross it off your list.

Once you have narrowed your sights to a particular home, loan type and amount, you will want to know if you can qualify for that specific loan. Later in this chapter, you will find four worksheets for this purpose. They cover the four major qualification methods: conventional, FHA, VA and DVA. Use the conventional loan worksheet for the Oregon Single Family Mortgage Purchase Program; for subsidized loans, such as the FHA 235 and the FmHA program, ask a loan officer to run the necessary calculations.

Calculating The Ballpark Estimate
Before the calculations begin, there is some information you will need to assemble. A quick call to a lending institution (ask for the Mortgage Loan Origination Department) or to a real estate agent should be all that is needed.

*What Is The Average Interest Rate On A New Loan?
If you know what type of loan you are interested in, such as a 1-year ARM, then ask for that specific rate. If you are "just looking", ask for an average rate for a fixed-rate 30-year loan and a range of rates for ARMs or GEMs. Remember too, that some loans have an introductory rate that is different from the note rate. Find out which rate will be used as a basis for qualification.

*Will Mortgage Insurance Be Required?
If so, what will the monthly premium be? To understand what mortgage insurance is and what it will cost, read the section that deals with it in the chapter on Loan Fees And Closing Costs. If your down payment (or equity, if you are financing) is less than 20 or 25% of the value of the home, mortgage insurance will probably be required by conventional lenders. While mortgage insurance is required on all FHA loans, it is handled in one of two ways. If you are considering FHA financing, be sure to study that chapter.

*What Would The Property Taxes Be For The Type Of Home You Would Like To Buy?
Real estate agents can give you a rough idea of what the annual cost would be for a certain size of home in a particular area.

Now you are ready to qualify yourself. Since most conventional lenders qualify buyers in two steps, known as the Housing Cost Ratio and the Total Debt Ratio, we will work through both procedures. Both ratios must fall within the acceptable limits in order for the borrower to qualify for the loan.

RULE OF THUMB FOR CONVENTIONAL LOAN QUALIFICATION

Many conventional lenders use the following percentages to determine loan eligibility;

* **monthly housing costs (principal, interest, mortgage insurance, property taxes, association dues, plus homeowner's insurance) may not exceed 28% of the borrower's gross monthly income, and in addition,**
* **total monthly debts (all of the above plus car payments, other loan payments, credit card expenses, alimony, child support etc.) may not exceed 36% of the borrower's gross monthly income.**

Note: 95% LTV conventional loans use 25% and 33%. Qualification percentages vary somewhat from lender to lender and from loan to loan. These quoted here are typical and will give a good overall picture of your financing capabilities.

Have paper and a calculator ready, take pen in hand and start computing:

THE BALLPARK ESTIMATE
HOUSING COST RATIO ("First Ratio")

STEP 1:   Determine your gross monthly income; that is, your income before taxes are deducted. For example, if you are paid weekly, multiply your weekly gross pay by 52, then divide by 12. For two-week pay periods, multiply by 26 before dividing by 12.

If your income is not in the form of a regular paycheck from an employer, or if part of your income is from bonuses, commissions or interest payments, read 'Is It Considered Income?' later in this chapter. Ditto if you are self-employed or have been employed at your present job less than two years.

STEP 2:   Multiply your gross monthly income by .28

Example: Gross monthly income of $2500 x .28 = $700.
This figure (the $700) in the example is the maximum
amount the bank will permit you to pay each month for
housing costs (principal, interest, property taxes plus
homeowner's insurance.)

STEP 3: From the answer obtained in Step 2, deduct
the cost per month of property taxes, homeowners'
insurance, association fees, if any, and mortgage insurance premium, if required). If you have been given
annual figures, divide by 12 to determine the monthly
cost.
Example:
          Add together: Property Taxes $100.
                        Homeowner's Insurance   14.
                        Mortgage Insurance   20.
                                                 $134.

          Deduct this from you answer to Step 2: $700.
                                                 − 134.
                                                 $566.

This is the maximum amount you will be permitted to
spend on monthly principal and interest payments.

STEP 4: Using the amortization chart in the Appendix
at the back of the book, find the factor that is based
upon the interest rate on a new loan and the term
(length) of the loan.

Example: If the interest rate on a new 30-year loan is
12.5%, the factor, according to the amortization chart
is 10.67. The factor would be the same for any 30-year
loan at 12.5%, whether fixed-rate, adjustable-rate or
graduated-payment.

STEP 5: Divide your answer to Step 3 by the factor in
Step 4, then move the decimal point three places to the
right.

Example: $566 ÷ 10.67 = 53.04592 ($53,045.92)

This gives you the maximum loan amount you may be qualified to borrow using the Housing Cost Ratio. But this ratio is only half the story! You must now see how you qualify using the Total Debt Service Ratio.

TOTAL DEBT SERVICE RATIO ('Second Ratio')
STEP 1: Multiply your gross monthly income by .36 (or by the percentage for the Total Debt Service Ratio given to you by the loan officer. It will be a number close to .36).
Example: $2500. X .36 = $900.

This is the total amount the lender will allow you to spend on housing costs (principal, interest, taxes and insurance) plus your regular monthly debts (car payments, other loans, alimony, child support, credit card payments, etc.).

STEP 2: Add up all of these monthly debts except principal and interest, then subtract the total from your answer to Step 1.

Example:

Property Taxes	$100.
Homeowner's Insurance	14.
Mortgage Insurance	20.
Car Payment	165.
Visa	50.
Total monthly debt service:	$349.

Then subtract: $900.
            −349.
            $551.

This is the maximum amount the lender will permit you to spend on monthly principal and interest payments, using the Total Debt Service Ratio.

STEP 3: Divide the answer to Step 2 by the factor you used in Steps 4 and 5 above.

Example: $551 ÷ 10.67 = 51.640112 ($51,640.11)

This is the maximum loan amount you are qualified to borrow on the basis of the Total Debt Service Ratio.

If the two ratios give different results, which is correct?
You can expect the maximum loan amounts to differ; it would be far more surprising to have a matched set of figures. But which will the lender use to determine how much you can borrow? Here are the guidelines:

If the maximum loan amount on the First Ratio exceeds that on the Second Ratio, the latter amount will usually be your top borrowing limit.

Example: In our calculations above, the maximum loan amounts for our borrower were as follows:

First Ratio	$53,045.92
Second Ratio	$51,640.11

The borrower's total monthly debts were higher than the lender would allow for a $53,045.92 loan. Therefore he or she could borrow only $51,640.11, the amount on the Second Ratio.

If the maximum loan amount on the Second Ratio exceeds that of the First Ratio, pat yourself on the back. Your total debts are less than the allowable limit. In this case, the First Ratio percentage may be raised, at the discretion of the lender, to 30% or even 32%, and the First Ratio figure will be used as the maximum loan amount.

Example: If, in our Second Ratio example above, the borrower had no car loan or monthly Visa payment, the total monthly debt service (excluding mortgage loan payment) would be only $134, instead of $349. After recalculating, we would find that the new maximum loan amount on the Second Ratio is $71,790. Quite a difference! Most lenders take this into account when qualifying borrowers. While a loan as high as $71,790 would probably not be permitted since it violates the First Ratio guidelines, a lender might be willing to bend the 28% rule to allow a 30% or 32% first ratio. That would give our borrower a maximum loan amount of $57,732 to $62,418.

Here is a worksheet to use as you calculate your own ballpark estimate:

BALLPARK ESTIMATE WORKSHEET

HOUSING COST RATIO:

Gross Monthly Income.................$.........
Multiply by............................. x .28 *

A. Maximum allowed for housing costs...$.........

Monthly cost of:
    Property Taxes..............$.........
    Homeowner's Insurance.....$.........
    Mortgage Insurance.........$.........
    Association Fees...........$.........

B. Total.....................$.........

Subtract Line B from Line A: Line A: $.........
              minus Line B: $.........

C. Maximum allowed for monthly
     principal and interest.............$.........

Loan Data:
    Interest Rate.........................%
    Term of loan...........................years
D. Amortization Factor..................
    (use chart in Appendix)

Divide Line C by Line D:
E. $ .... ÷ .... = $.........

Line E is the maximum loan amount determined by the Housing Cost Ratio.

*   For 95% LTV Conventional Loans use .25

189

TOTAL DEBT SERVICE RATIO:

Multiply your gross monthly income by .36: *

    Gross monthly income. . . . . $. . . . .

                                           x .36 *

                                                      ——————

F. Maximum allowed for housing costs
     plus total debts. . . . . $. . . . .

Total monthly debts:

    Property taxes. . . . . $. . . . .

    Homeowner's Insurance. . . . . $. . . . .

    Mortgage Insurance. . . . . $. . . . .

    Association Fees. . . . . $. . . . .

    Car Payment. . . . . $. . . . .

    Other Loan Payments. . . . . . . $. . . . .

    Total Credit Card Payment . . . $. . . . .

    Alimony/Child Support. . . . . . $. . . . .

    Other monthly payments. . . . . $. . . . .

                                    ——————

G. Total monthly debts. . . . . . . $. . . . .

Subtract Line G from Line F: Line F: $. . . . .

                            minus Line G: $. . . . .

                                            ——————

H. Maximum principal and
     and interest payments. . . . . $. . . . .

Divide Line H by the Amortization Factor (Line D)

I. $. . . . . . . ÷ . . . . = $. . . . .

Line I is the maximum loan amount as determined by the Total Debt Service Ratio. Study the instructions preceeding this worksheet to interpret the results of your calculations.

*   For 95% LTV Conventional Loans use .33

Getting Down To Specifics
The estimate above will get you into the ballpark. When you are ready for the last inning of the financing game, you will want more specific information. Use the following worksheets when you know the size of loan you need and the particular home you hope to finance.

They will answer the ultimate question, "Can I afford it?", or in other words, "Do I qualify for this loan?". You may have to try various loan programs, at different interest rates or terms, until you find one that fits.

Four worksheets are included, for four different types of loans. The conventional method is a basic one, with a variation on the theme used by FHA. VA and DVA use quite different techniques. All are very straightforward and easy to use.

You will find that there are extenuating circumstances in many financing situations. If your calculations show that you do not qualify for the loan, don't be discouraged. After all, you are not a member of the loan committee which will grant the loan or reject your application. A lender may look at your financial picture in an entirely different light. Loan officers are very adept at helping borrowers find hidden assets they had no idea could be used in their favor. Quite often, a loan officer will suggest a small change that will make a significant difference in the loan application.

Is it considered income?
When using a qualification worksheet, the question of income arises. What may or may not be considered income? May bonuses, alimony, child support, and interest earned from stocks, bonds or notes be counted in the qualifying ratios? Lenders use the terms "sustained", "stable" or "steady" to define income that is acceptable for this purpose. If an applicant received a $20,000 bonus last year, it will be counted as income only if the bonus has been that large in previous years and is certain to continue.

A man I sold a home to a few years ago, regularly received a $5,000 bonus each December. Just before he applied for the loan, he was promoted to the position of district manager. He was told that he could expect a higher bonus, one between $8,000 and $12,000, depending upon the company's sales. The loan committee refused to allow the bonus to be included as income for two reasons: first, the employer would not sign a letter of guarantee that the bonus would be paid, and second, the applicant was new to his job and could not show a steady string of such bonuses for this work. The irony of the situation was that, had he not accepted the new position, the loan committee might have included his $5,000 bonus as income, since he had consistently earned one for the past several years.

There is no standard guideline for non-salary income. Your loan officer can cite institutional policy but much will depend upon the loan committee's view of your overall financial picture. Self-employed applicants often have a more difficult time in proving a stable income. For this and other kinds of irregular income, adequate documentation is essential. So in filling out the worksheets, consider only the income that is steady and predictable. Everything else is just frosting: nice if you can use it but don't count on anything other than plain cake.

Conventional Qualification Worksheet

Loan Amount _____ at _____ % interest.

Applicant's gross monthly income $ _____

Spouse's gross monthly income $ _____

A.   TOTAL GROSS MONTHLY INCOME $ _____

Monthly Housing Expense:

Loan Payment

   (principal & interest; see Appendix I) $ _____

Estimated monthly property tax $ _____

Estimated monthly homeowner's insurance $ _____

Private mortgage insurance premium, if any $ _____

Association fees, if any $ _____

B.   TOTAL MONTHLY HOUSING COST $ _____

Total Monthly Debts:

Housing cost (Line B) $ _____

Automobile loan payment $ _____

Other loan payments $ _____

Child support/alimony $ _____

Credit card payments $ _____

Other monthly obligations $ _____

C.   TOTAL MONTHLY DEBT SERVICE $ _____

For this worksheet we will use 28% and 36% for the two ratios. If the particular loan you are applying for has different requirements, use the percentages suggested by your loan officer. Remember that you must qualify for both ratios.

HOUSING COST RATIO: Line B must not exceed 28% of Line A.
   Line B ($) divided by Line A ($)
   must equal .28 or less to qualify.

TOTAL DEBT SERVICE RATIO: Line C must not exceed 36% of Line A.
   Line C ($) divided by Line A ($)
   must equal .36 or less to qualify.

If you fail to qualify according to this worksheet, check with a loan officer. Rules may sometimes be bent if the overall financial picture is sound.

FHA QUALIFICATION WORKSHEET

Loan Amount _____ **at** ___ **% interest.**

Monthly Housing Expense:

Monthly payment (P&I; see Appendix I)	$ _____
FHA mortgage insurance (unless paid in full at closing)	$ _____
Estimated monthly property tax	$ _____
Estimated monthly fire insurance	$ _____
Estimated monthly heat and utilities	$ _____
Maintenance	$ _____
A. TOTAL HOUSING EXPENSE	$ _____

Gross monthly income	$ _____
Less Federal Tax	$ _____
B. NET EFFECTIVE INCOME	$ _____

Monthly Debt:

Total housing expense (Line A)	$ _____
State income tax	$ _____
Social Security payment (7.15% of income to $42,000; if self-employed, use 12.3%)	$ _____
Life insurance premium	$ _____
Retirement fund	$ _____
Automobile loan payment	$ _____
Other loan payments	$ _____
All installment payments (that will last 12 months or more)	$ _____
C. TOTAL MONTHLY DEBT	$ _____

FHA GUIDELINES:
Line A may not exceed 38% of Line B:
   Line A ($) divided by Line B ($) must equal .38 or less
for the applicant to qualify.

And Line C may not exceed 53% of Line B:
   Line C ($) divided by Line B ($) must equal .53 or less
for the applicant to qualify.

These are the official guidelines. The percentages are sometimes stretched when the overall financial picture is sound. If you do not qualify according to this worksheet, ask a loan officer to review your figures.

VA QUALIFICATION WORKSHEET

Loan amount_____ at ___% interest.

Mortgage payment (P&I, see Appendix 1)	$ _____
Estimated monthly property tax	$ _____
Estimated monthly fire insurance	$ _____
Monthly maintenance expense	$ _____
Monthly heat and utilities	$ _____
A. TOTAL MONTHLY SHELTER COST	$ _____

Monthly obligations (over 6 months):	$ _____
Automobile payment	$ _____
Other loan payments	$ _____
Credit card payments	$ _____
Other	$ _____
B. TOTAL MONTHLY DEBTS	$ _____

C. GROSS MONTHLY INCOME	$ _____

Federal Income Tax (monthly)	$ ___
State Income Tax (monthly)	$ ___
Social Security (monthly)	$ ___
Other payroll deductions	$ ___
D. TOTAL DEDUCTIONS	$ ___

CORRECTION

Please note:
page 195 should read
LINE C MINUS LINE D
instead of ADD LINE C
TO LINE D

Add Line C	
to Line D	$ _____
Net Take-Home Pay	$ _____
Subtract the sum of A plus B	$ _____
E. BALANCE AVAILABLE	$ _____

Compare Line E. to the chart below based on family size (vet + spouse + dependents). Line E must be equal to or greater than the chart amount in order to qualify for the loan.

single vet	$443
family of 2	$697
family of 3	$847
family of 4	$941
family of 5	$1025
add $75 per member up to a family of 7	

To check a second way, add the monthly mortgage loan payment, property taxes and insurance (PITI) to Line B. Divide your answer by Line C. The answer must be less than .41 to qualify.

DVA QUALIFICATION WORKSHEET

Note that DVA uses "net income", your monthly income after taxes have been deducted.

Amount of loan _____ **at** ____ **% interest.**

NET INCOME PER MONTH

Veteran	$ _____
Spouse	$ _____
Other income	$ _____
A. Total Monthly Income	$ _____

MONTHLY PAYMENTS

DVA mortgage payment (See Appendix I)	$ _____
2nd mortgage payment, if any	$ _____
Child support/alimony	$ _____
Automobile payment	$ _____
Food (DVA uses figure of $100 per person)	$ _____
Utilities (gas, elec., tel./DVA uses $150)	$ 150.00
Total Monthly (use 25% of your net income)	$ _____
Other monthly payments	$ _____
B. Total Monthly Payments	$ _____

C. Difference Remaining
        (Line A minus Line B) $ _____

Line C must equal 10% or more of line A for the applicant to qualify.

CHAPTER 28

Loan Processing:
From Application To Approval

Most loans are processed by banks, S&Ls, mortgage companies and mortgage brokers. These institutions take applications not only for conventional loans but also for some types of government-backed financing such as FHA, Federal VA and Oregon Single Family Mortgage Purchase Program loans. Not every lending institution handles all types of loans, so be sure to choose one that services the particular program you have in mind.

If you have decided to apply for an Oregon DVA loan, a Federal Land Bank loan or a Farmers Home Administration loan, you must contact these agencies directly.

How To Choose A 'Good' Lender
Lending institutions are kept in check by governmental regulations and common-sense banking practices. As a result, there is great similarity between them in the mechanics of loan processing. That does not, however, mean that all lending institutions are equal.

Variations in interest rates and loan fees are often a factor in a borrower's choice. If Lender A is offering fixed-rate 30-year loans at 12%, while Lenders B and C offer no less than 13% for similar loans, then it might be wise to talk to Lender A. But do pay close attention to word-of-mouth recommendations. A conscientious loan officer and a lending institution that processes its loan applications efficiently are worth valuable consideration.

"WHO THE HELL IS FANNIE MAE?"
or
WHY YOU CAN'T ARGUE WITH A LOAN OFFICER . . . AND WIN

I once watched an inexperienced loan officer drown a prospective borrower in a sea of unfamiliar words. The monologue was peppered with unexplained phrases such as "cap rate", "GEM features", and "negative amortization". Then the speaker began extolling the virtues of Fannie Mae, noting with obvious satisfaction that the condominium to be purchased met with her approval. The applicant, by this time, had reached a point of complete exasperation. He jumped up and demanded, "Who the hell is Fannie Mae anyway? And why should she give a damn about my condo?"

Fannie Mae commands respect in lending circles. So do her sidekicks Ginnie Mae and Freddie Mac. These three, properly named the Federal National Mortgage Association (FNMA), the Government National Mortgage Association (GNMA), and the Federal Home Loan Mortgage Corporation (FHLMC) respectively, are agencies which buy loans from lending institutions. This is what is known as the secondary market.

Lenders sell their loans on the secondary market to investors who pay cash, which can, in turn, be used to finance other loans. An institution which lacks sufficient investors will be limited in its ability to service the market. Lenders cannot continue to make loans without available funds. The agencies mentioned above are three of the major investors in home mortgage loans. Insurance companies also buy heavily on the secondary market. Loans are sold in groups, or blocks, worth millions of dollars, and so the investors are usually large corporations or syndicates of individual investors.

Loan Guidelines
Investors are very fussy when it comes to buying loans. With that much money behind them, they can call the shots. Each investor issues a set of guidelines for the loans to be purchased and lenders must follow these to the letter if they hope to sell the loan to that buyer.

Lenders are certainly anxious to sell! As one loan officer put it, "The only good loan is a saleable one. An even better loan is one we've already sold."

Because Fannie Mae has immense buying capability, the FNMA guidelines are treated with almost as much reverence as the Ten Commandments. Lenders cannot afford to ignore them. That is why, if Fannie Mae (or another investor) specifically requires mortgage insurance on all loans over 80% LTV, a borrower's tearful plea for no PMI will fall on deaf ears. That, in a nutshell, is why you can't argue with a loan officer, and win.

Non-Conforming Loans
But surely, you say, there is an investor somewhere with a different taste in loans. Yes, that's quite true. Not all guidelines are the same. But common sense and good banking practices prevail. Investors will not go too far out on a limb and risk buying shaky loans.

There is one FNMA guideline that is commonly ignored by other investors. That is the maximum loan amount on any loan purchased. Both FNMA and FHLMC have a current limit of $133,250 but this will increase from time to time. (GNMA buys FHA, VA and FmHA loans, all of which have their own limits.) Who finances the $500,000 properties? Other investors have stepped in to fill this need and so lenders are able to offer larger loans, known in the trade as Jumbo Loans. These, and any other loans that do not follow Fannie Mae or Freddie Mac guidelines are called "non-conforming" loans. They will still be sold, but to investors who play by different rules.

Who Will Buy My Loan?
When a bank, savings & loan, or mortgage company sells your loan, you will not feel a thing. Unless you happen to ask, you will not know that an investor has purchased it. Your lender will continue to receive your monthly payment and will service the loan just as though it had not been sold.

Mortgage Brokers
Do not confuse this with the practices of a mortgage broker. Mortgage brokers process loan applications for other lenders. They do all of the "up front" work of the lending institution that is actually making the loan. Sometimes borrowers are surprised to find, at closing, that the loan documents are from XYZ Bank when their only contact has been with ABC Services, a mortgage broker. After closing, XYZ Bank will service the loan, paying a fee to the broker who handled the initial stages. The loan may then be sold on the secondary market by XYZ. Mortgage brokers have been an asset to the lending market by offering a wide assortment of loans that are not available from local lenders.

"May We Pick Up The Check On Tuesday?"
Many borrowers are surprised to learn that it takes from four to eight weeks to obtain new financing. The largest portion of that time is spent in verifying the borrower's credit information and in collecting data needed by the loan committee in making its decision. Once the pertinent facts and documents have been assembled, a loan committee needs very little time to approve the loan, from several hours to a few days at most.

You can accelerate the process by giving the loan officer a head start on the paperwork. If you arrive at the loan application interview (otherwise known as the 'loan app') with all the necessary information in hand, the processing time for your loan will be considerably shorter, closer to the four- rather than the eight-week mark.

Applying For An Assumption
For many loan assumptions, buyers are required to make formal application, just as if they were applying for a new loan. In such a case, the same information and documents will be needed. While most lenders do not require a new appraisal, some do. If so, a check for this amount will be collected at that time.

Preparing For Loan Application
Here is a checklist to get you ready for your meeting with the loan officer. 200

LOAN APPLICATION CHECKLIST

I. **Your checkbook,** to pay for the credit report and appraisal (these must be paid for at loan app)

II. **Information about the home:**
(eliminate items 1 and 2 if refinancing)
1. a legible and complete copy of the sales agreement
2. a copy of the earnest money check or note
3. a 'trio' (from your real estate agent or title insurance company) or other documents showing information and legal description
4. name and phone number of person who can give appraiser access to the home
5. for FHA and VA loans: copies of heat and utility bills for the past 12 months or signed statement from seller showing costs

III. **Personal information** (for applicant and spouse if both incomes are to be counted or if both will take title to the property):
1. current home address and phone number
2. previous home address for the past four years
3. birth dates
4. Social Security numbers
5. name and address of current employers
6. name and address of previous employers (past two years)
7. for veterans' loans (VA, FHA/VA, DVA) a copy of your discharge paper (DD214)
8. for VA loans: name and address of your nearest living relative

IV. **Assets and Liabilities** (for applicant and spouse as above):
1. current gross salary (before deductions)
2. list and amounts of paycheck deductions
3. income for the past three years (from all sources)

4. if you work on commission: federal income tax returns for the past three years
5. if you are (or were) self-employed: federal income tax returns plus profit and loss statements for the past three years (a CPA's signature is often required)
6. record of benefits received, such as social security, disability, veterans' benefits
7. names, addresses and account numbers of all banks, S&Ls, credit unions etc. where you have a savings or checking account plus the approximate balance of each account
8. names, addresses and account numbers of all your credit cards and credit accounts, plus the balance and monthly payments required on each
   (this includes everything from Mastercard and Visa, to department store credit cards and your charge account at the local hardware store)
9. names, addresses, account numbers, monthly payments and balance of any current or previous loans, such as other mortgage loans, car loans, student loans, etc.
10. record of any stocks or bonds that you own plus name and address of brokerage firm that can verify holdings
11. proof of any assets such as cash value life insurance or retirement fund
12. if you own rental property: copies of lease agreements plus certification of expenses such as mortgage loan payments, taxes, etc.
13. if you receive or pay alimony or child support: a copy of the divorce decree and deposit receipts or other proof
14. an estimate of the value of all your personal property: household goods, clothing, jewelry, hobby equipment, etc.
15. information about any bankruptcy or judgments

What To Expect From The 'Loan App'

Once you have assembled the vast bundle of necessary information, make an appointment to see the loan officer you have chosen. Because the application forms are complicated and confusing, loan officers prefer to fill out the form with the prospective borrower sitting close by.

During the 'loan app', the loan officer will discuss the various loan possibilities and will run calculations to see if you qualify for the size and type of loan you want. You will be given a written estimate of your closing costs and the monthly payment figures. The loan officer will then fill in the application form and will have you sign it. At the same time, you will also be asked to sign form letters to your employer and to the banks, credit unions or S&Ls where you have an account, requesting verification of employment and funds.

You must also leave a check for the cost of the credit report and appraisal (usually a total of $175 to $225). This is not refundable, even if the loan is not approved, and that is why loan officers take time to qualify you first. It should be noted that even if a loan officer's preliminary calculations indicate that you are qualified, the loan may be denied by the loan committee. Results of the credit report, the employment and financial verification, and the appraisal can darken an otherwise rosy picture.

A Timetable For Loan Processing

You've done your part. From here on, you are at the mercy of the loan officer, the U.S. Postal Service, the credit reporting agency, the appraiser, your bank and your employer's payroll department. How quickly you receive your loan approval will depend upon the speed and efficiency of all of the above. Of course, applicants with out-of-state employers or bank accounts can expect a longer wait than those whose verification letters are mailed to local addresses. However, in general, the timetable for a typical new loan would be like this:

Day 1	Loan application
Days 2 — 7	Financial and employment verification letters sent by lender
	Credit report and appraisal ordered by lender
Days 6 — 14	Appraiser inspects home (written appraisal sent to lender within one week)
Days 15 — 28	Appraisal, credit report and completed verification letters received by lender

When all the documents have been received, the loan officer will examine the data and will put together a 'package' for the loan committee. A weak spot may have appeared in your financial picture or there may be an area that needs better explanation. For example, your credit report might show a current car loan, even though you paid it in full last month. Or perhaps your company's verification letter did not mention the $20,000 bonus you customarily earn. In these cases, the loan officer will ask you for additional documentation or proof, such as a letter from the automobile credit company, or a correction of the employment verification.

As soon as your loan officer has assembled a loan package that will present your strongest possible case, it is sent to the loan committee. Usually within 1 to 4 days, you will hear one of three answers:
* your loan has been approved
   or
* your loan has been conditionally approved (approved only if you agree to accept certain conditions)
   or
* your loan has been denied

Even if your loan has not been approved, most lenders will allow the package to be resubmitted if new supporting information has been received. However, your loan application will have a much better chance of survival if all the weak spots are fortified before the loan committee finds them.

Adequate Funds To Close

"Don't worry, I'll dig up the down payment somewhere," is a statement that guarantees a quick exit from any loan office. A borrower who cannot show sufficient funds for the down payment and closing costs will not get a loan.

That sounds ridiculously elementary; of course you need to have enough money for closing. But has that money been sitting in your bank account since loan application? Or is it somewhere else at the moment? Your lender would like to know.

If the financial information on your application clearly shows where the closing funds will be coming from, and if this amount is in cash or in an asset that is readily converted to cash (bonds, for instance), there will be no problem. But if your bank accounts do not show enough money to close and no other obvious assets are present, you will have to offer proof of sufficient funds before you will receive loan approval.

Gift Letters And Borrowed Down Payment

Perhaps a relative will be giving you money for the down payment. If so, the lender will want a 'gift letter' from the donor, stating clearly that this is a gift and repayment is not required.

If, however, someone will be lending you the money, the loan officer will need to have some documentation of the loan, explaining just how and when the money is to be repaid. These private loan payments will be included in the qualifying calculations and may lower your borrowing limit.

Countdown To Closing

After you have received loan approval, your direct contact with the loan officer is over. The loan processing department prepares the documents that will be needed and sends them to the escrow company chosen to handle the closing. Even if you are simply refinancing your present home, there will still be an escrow closing.

First we'll tackle the issue of closing costs.

CHAPTER 29

Loan Costs And Escrow Closing

Financing a home can be an expensive proposition. Many prospective borrowers are dumbfounded when they notice the bottom line of the closing cost estimate prepared by their loan officer. In today's financing realm, it is not at all unusual for a borrower to pay loan fees, closing costs and reserves of 7% or 8% of the loan amount. A buydown and discount points can push this total even higher. Add to this the down payment and you will see why many buyers are priced out of the market before their application even gets to loan committee.

It is wise to plan ahead for these costs before finding the home of your dreams. If you realize that, for example, $5,000 or $6,000 of your cash reserves may have to be used for closing costs on a new loan, then you can make an informed decision about buying or refinancing a home.

Here is a chart which shows the types of fees customarily charged for different types of financing. The exact amounts differ from loan to loan; where I have included a figure, it is a fairly standard amount. The blank spaces to the right of the chart are for your personal use, to be filled with information gathered from lenders. Of course, when you do apply for a loan, or have a pre-application conference, your loan officer will supply a detailed estimate of your closing costs. This chart is simply an overall view of financing expenses, to let you know in advance what to expect.

CLOSING COSTS

	Conventional Loan	Conventional Refinance	FHA Loan	VA Loan	DVA Loan	Assumption	Land Sales Contract	Estimated Loan Costs
Appraisal Fee	★	★	★	★		●		
Credit Report	★	★	★	★	★	★		
Loan Fee/Assumption Fee	★	★	★	★	★	★		
VA Funding Fee				★				
Discount Points	●	●	★	★				
Buydown Fee	●	●	●	●				
Mortgage Insurance Premium	●	●	★					
Underwriting Fee	★	★	★	★				
Tax Service Fee	★	★	★	★	★			
Survey Fee	●	●	●	●	●			
Inspection Fee	●	●	●	●				
Mortgagee's Title Insurance	★	★	★	★	★			
Interest Payment	★	★	★	★	★	★		
Down Payment	★		★	●	★	★	★	
Homeowner's Insurance	★	★	★	★	★	★	★	
Tax Reserves	●	●	★	★		●	●	
Tax Pro-rates	★	★	★	★	★	★	★	
Escrow Fee	★	★	★	★	★	★	★	
Recording Fees	★	★	★	★	★	★	★	
Transfer Tax	●	●	●	●	●	●	●	●
Owner's Title Insurance Policy	★	★	★	★	★	★	★	
Real Estate Commission	★		★	★	★	★	★	

★ Fee usually charged

● Fee may be charged

Here is an explanation of the items found on the chart. Many have names that are thoroughly mystifying to even the most seasoned borrowers.

Appraisal Fee:
This fee is paid at time of loan application, to cover the cost of appraising the home. Estimate for a single-family home: $250 for a conventional appraisal, $175 for VA, $250 for an FHA appraisal in the Portland metro area, $200 elsewhere.

Credit Report:
Paid at the time of loan application, a credit report on the borrower can cost from $45 to $65 dollars, sometimes more if from out-of-state.

Loan Fee:
The fee charged by the lender. It is usually expressed as a percentage of the loan amount. Conventional loan fees today vary from about 2% to 4% (more if discount points are included in the figure). The fees on government-backed loans are usually lower (around 1%).

VA Funding Fee:
A 1% fee, in addition to the 1% loan fee, that is charged for VA loans. This fee supports the loan guaranty program.

Discount Points:
These have been discussed in the chapter on Buydowns, as well as in the FHA and VA chapters. One discount point equals one percent of the loan amount.

Buydown Fee:
The interest rate may be lowered through the use of a buydown. Fees vary considerably. For more information, see the chapter on Buydowns.

Mortgage Insurance Premium:
Varies with type and amount of loan. See a discussion of this in the Conventional Loans section and also in the chapter on FHA loans. The first year's premium is required on conventional financing. Occasionally an extra month or two of premium will be collected at closing if the first payment will not be due immediately.

Underwriting Fee:
Also known as the Document Preparation Fee, this covers the lender's cost to draw up the necessary documents. Allow $100.

Tax Service Fee:
The fee to provide the lender with an accurate report of the property tax status (delinquent, paid in full, etc.). The seller must pay this on all FHA loans. Estimate $54.

Survey Fee:
For new construction and most loans over $100,000 the lenders require foundation surveys. Estimate $65.

Inspection Fee:
If repairs are required by the FHA or VA appraiser, the property must be re-inspected. Cost: $30.

Mortgagee's Title Insurance:
Most lenders except DVA require what is known as an ALTA policy. DVA requires a standard mortgagee's policy. See rate table in Appendix.

Interest Payment:
Although interest is paid at the end of each month, the first monthly payment may not be scheduled to start for 45 days or so after closing. Therefore the first interest payment will be collected at closing, based on the number of days remaining in that month.

Down Payment:
While not actually a closing cost, it is a cash payment that is collected at or before closing.

Homeowner's Insurance:
One year to 14 months of insurance must be paid at closing. Value must be equal to or greater than the loan amount.

Tax Reserves:
Property tax reserves are required on most government loans and conventional loans over 80% LTV. Estimate 9 months' worth.

Tax Pro-Rates:
In almost every transaction one party (the buyer or the seller) must reimburse the other for property taxes. The tax bill is due each year on November 15th. This bill covers the one-year period from the previous July 1st to the following June 30th. If the seller pays the bill in full in November but sells the home two months later, on January 15th, the buyer will owe the seller five and one-half months worth of taxes, since they have been paid through June 30th of that year.

If the closing were to take place on September 15th, the seller would be responsible for the taxes up to that date. Since the new tax bill will not be printed until November, there is no way for the seller to pay the county for the period from July 1st through September 15th. The county will not accept funds until the bill has been established. Therefore, the seller will reimburse the buyer at closing for two and one-half months of taxes, based on the previous year's rate.

Escrow Fee:
The fee charged by the escrow company for the services of the escrow officer in preparing the closing documents and conducting the escrow closing. Varies with sales price (or loan amount for a refinance) and differs slightly from company to company. Fee is split between buyer and seller except for VA loans where seller pays entire fee. Estimate a total escrow fee of $60.00 plus $3.00 per $1,000 of sales price; on amounts over $100,000 estimate $.75 per $1,000. Many escrow companies offer a reduction for refinance closings (count on 25% discount). There is often a slightly lower fee on new construction.

Recording Fees:
The cost for recording the deed and the loan documents varies slightly from county to county and is based upon the number of pages recorded. Estimate $20 to $35 for a fixed-rate loan or basic land sales contract, $40 to $50 for a complicated loan, such as an ARM.

Transfer Tax:
For property in Washington county only. Tax is $.50 per $1,000 for both buyer and seller. Not charged for refinances.

Owner's Title Insurance Policy:
Premium paid by the seller to provide insurance for the purchaser against possible defects of title. See table of costs in Appendix.

Real Estate Commission:
Paid by the seller at closing.

THE ESCROW CLOSING

In Oregon the closing is customarily held at the office of a title insurance company. The procedure is the same whether you are buying, selling or refinancing your present home. The closing is conducted by an escrow officer, the person responsible for assembling the necessary documents, calculating the buyers' and seller's cost sheets, carrying out the lender's instructions, recording the deed and loan documents, and disbursing the proceeds.

By law, escrow officers must remain neutral; they may not side with one party over another. Their job is to handle the paperwork and funds in an impartial manner. To preserve this neutrality they must follow only written instructions that have been signed by both parties or by the lender and borrower. If a buyer calls to say, "I want you to hold back $50 until the seller repairs a crack in the ceiling", the escrow agent is powerless to comply, unless the request is presented in writing and agreed to by the seller as well. An escrow officer may not attempt to negotiate a sticky point in a transaction; that is what real estate agents are able to do. For serious difficulties, ask your attorney to smooth the path.

Closing Procedure
Closings in Oregon are less formal than in many eastern states where buyers, sellers and their attorneys face each other across a formidable conference table.

Here, when closing day arrives, buyers and sellers make separate appointments with the escrow officer. Each party meets at a different time, to review and sign the documents and, in the case of the buyer, to bring in a certified check for the down payment and closing costs. (The escrow officer will advise the buyer of the required amount a day or two in advance.) When both parties have signed, the escrow officer will send the loan documents to the lender for a last-minute check. Once the lender approves, the trust deed (or mortgage) will be delivered to the county courthouse to be recorded. The lender will issue a check to fund the loan and will send it to the escrow officer. Finally the warranty deed signed by the seller, giving title to the buyer, will be recorded.

The Services Of An Attorney
Should an attorney advise you or represent you at closing? In eastern and midwestern states, where title insurance is not frequently used, the answer to this question would be a definite "yes". There, attorneys are needed to do a title search of the property, assuring the buyer that the title is good and marketable. A friend of mine who owns a home in Ohio discovered to her dismay that someone else owned her entire front yard and wanted an exhorbitant price for it. She had bought the home without a title search.

Here, in Oregon, the use of title insurance is customary. The seller provides it for the buyer and the borrower buys a policy for the lender, to protect against unforeseen defects of title. The title insurance company conducts a title search and issues a preliminary report to both buyers and sellers. Any surprise encumbrances should be called to the attention of your real estate agent, escrow officer or attorney before closing. For example, the preliminary report may show a lien against the property that neither the buyer nor seller knew about. Unless the lien can be removed, it must be paid off at closing, the closing must be postponed until the problem can be resolved, or the buyer must agree to allow that lien to remain. If, as in the case of my friend, you later discover that a stranger owns your yard, the title insurance company will use the necessary legal means to correct the situation, unless, of course, you were advised in the preliminary report that you were not purchasing that part of the property.

With title insurance, an attorney is not absolutely essential for a simple transaction. Most buyers and sellers in Oregon do not consult an attorney for the purchase, sale or refinancing of a home, except in the case of seller-financing, sweat equity or an unusual agreement between the parties. However, loan documents can be overwhelming in their complexity. If you feel uncertain about any phase of the transaction, from the purchase offer to the closing papers, do not hesitate to seek legal advice.

Disbursement Of Funds
The proceeds from the closing will be disbursed by the escrow officer after the documents have been recorded. Because the post-signing activities take time, sellers should expect a wait of one to several days before receiving a check. Lenders often want 24 to 48 hours to review the signed loan papers, and there may be a day's delay in transmitting the papers to the county for recording. Discuss the timing with your escrow officer in advance so that you will know what to expect.

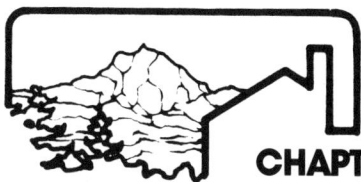

CHAPTER 30

A Final Word

Real estate agents have been known to feel particularly proud of themselves for putting together transactions that seem impossible. It is satisfying to see buyers enjoying homes they never knew they could afford, and it is equally rewarding to have helped sell a home that, by rights, should be renting a long-term space in the pages of the local multiple listing book. Knowledge of the wide range of possible financing methods can indeed work miracles.

On the other hand, it is frustrating to see homeowners tied to a loan that is wrong for them. Home-ownership should be a pleasure, not a monstrous drain on the checkbook. Even when interest rates are high, there are financing choices to be made and a sensible plan of action to be followed. Choose carefully; surely no home is worth the agonies suffered with a foreclosure sale.

In the previous chapters we have looked at the many kinds of loans available today in Oregon, some desirable, others of questionable value. I have tossed facts and figures at you, added a healthy dose of personal opinion, and offered guidelines for choosing the best possible financing. If the book has given you hope that there is a loan for you, if it has steered you away from the wrong type of financing for your needs, or if it has helped you think of creative ways to market a home, then I've accomplished my goal. Good luck!

APPENDIX I

Loan Amortization Schedule

Use this chart to determine what your monthly principal and interest payment will be. Real estate loan payments are amortized over the term of the loan. That is, the payments are calculated to include the correct amount of principal and interest so that the loan balance will be zero at the end of the term.

Step 1: Find the applicable interest rate in the top row.

Step 2: Find the term of the loan in the column on the left.

Step 3: Trace down the rate column and across the term row to the square where the two meet. Remember this factor.

Step 4: Move the decimal point in your loan amount three places to the left. Example: $57,850. becomes 57.850.

Step 5: Multiply this number by the factor you have found on the chart.

Example: A 12% loan with a term of 30 years would have a factor of 10.29 according to the chart. If the loan balance is $57,850, we would multiply 57.850 by 10.29 and find that our monthly payment (principal and interest) would be $595.28.

years	8.00	8.25	8.50	8.75	9.00	9.25	9.50	9.75	10.00	10.25	10.50 %
1	86.99	87.10	87.22	87.34	87.45	87.57	87.68	87.80	87.92	88.03	88.15
	45.23	45.34	45.46	45.57	45.68	45.80	45.91	46.03	46.14	46.26	46.38
	31.34	31.45	31.57	31.68	31.80	31.92	32.03	32.15	32.27	32.38	32.50
	24.41	24.53	24.65	24.77	24.89	25.00	25.12	25.24	25.36	25.48	25.60
5	20.28	20.40	20.52	20.64	20.76	20.88	21.00	21.12	21.25	21.37	21.49
	17.53	17.66	17.78	17.90	18.03	18.15	18.27	18.40	18.53	18.65	18.78
	15.59	15.71	15.84	15.96	16.09	16.22	16.34	16.47	16.60	16.73	16.86
	14.14	14.26	14.39	14.52	14.65	14.78	14.91	15.04	15.17	15.31	15.44
	13.02	13.15	13.28	13.41	13.54	13.68	13.81	13.94	14.08	14.21	14.35
10	12.13	12.27	12.40	12.53	12.67	12.80	12.94	13.08	13.22	13.35	13.49
	11.42	11.55	11.69	11.82	11.96	12.10	12.24	12.38	12.52	12.66	12.80
	10.82	10.96	11.10	11.24	11.38	11.52	11.66	11.81	11.95	12.10	12.24
	10.33	10.47	10.61	10.75	10.90	11.04	11.19	11.33	11.48	11.63	11.78
	9.91	10.06	10.20	10.34	10.49	10.64	10.78	10.93	11.08	11.23	11.38
15	9.56	9.70	9.85	9.99	10.14	10.29	10.44	10.59	10.75	10.90	11.05
	9.25	9.40	9.54	9.69	9.85	10.00	10.15	10.30	10.46	10.62	10.77
	8.98	9.13	9.28	9.43	9.59	9.74	9.90	10.05	10.21	10.37	10.53
	8.75	8.90	9.05	9.21	9.36	9.52	9.68	9.84	10.00	10.16	10.32
	8.55	8.70	8.85	9.01	9.17	9.33	9.49	9.65	9.81	9.98	10.14
20	8.36	8.52	8.68	8.84	9.00	9.16	9.32	9.49	9.65	9.82	9.98
	8.20	8.36	8.52	8.68	8.85	9.01	9.17	9.34	9.51	9.68	9.85
	8.06	8.22	8.38	8.55	8.71	8.88	9.04	9.21	9.38	9.55	9.73
	7.93	8.10	8.26	8.43	8.59	8.76	8.93	9.10	9.27	9.44	9.62
	7.82	7.98	8.15	8.32	8.49	8.66	8.83	9.00	9.17	9.35	9.52
25	7.72	7.88	8.05	8.22	8.39	8.56	8.74	8.91	9.09	9.26	9.44
	7.63	7.79	7.96	8.13	8.31	8.48	8.66	8.83	9.01	9.19	9.37
	7.54	7.71	7.88	8.06	8.23	8.41	8.58	8.76	8.94	9.12	9.30·
	7.47	7.64	7.81	7.99	8.16	8.34	8.52	8.70	8.88	9.06	9.25
	7.40	7.57	7.75	7.92	8.10	8.28	8.46	8.64	8.82	9.01	9.19
30	7.34	7.51	7.69	7.87	8.05	8.23	8.41	8.59	8.78	8.96	9.15

	10.75	11.00	11.25	11.50	11.75	12.00	12.25	12.50	12.75	13.00	13.25 %
1	88.27	88.38	88.50	88.62	88.73	88.85	88.97	89.08	89.20	89.32	89.43
	46.49	46.61	46.72	46.84	46.96	47.07	47.19	47.31	47.42	47.54	47.66
	32.62	32.74	32.86	32.98	33.10	33.21	33.33	33.45	33.57	33.69	33.81
	25.72	25.85	25.97	26.09	26.21	26.33	26.46	26.58	26.70	26.83	26.95
5	21.62	21.74	21.87	21.99	22.12	22.24	22.37	22.50	22.63	22.75	22.88
	18.91	19.03	19.16	19.29	19.42	19.55	19.68	19.81	19.94	20.07	20.21
	16.99	17.12	17.25	17.39	17.52	17.65	17.79	17.92	18.06	18.19	18.33
	15.57	15.71	15.84	15.98	16.12	16.25	16.39	16.53	16.67	16.81	16.95
	14.49	14.63	14.76	14.90	15.04	15.18	15.33	15.47	15.61	15.75	15.90
10	13.63	13.78	13.92	14.06	14.20	14.35	14.49	14.64	14.78	14.93	15.08
	12.95	13.09	13.24	13.38	13.53	13.68	13.83	13.98	14.13	14.28	14.43
	12.39	12.54	12.68	12.83	12.98	13.13	13.29	13.44	13.59	13.75	13.90
	11.92	12.08	12.23	12.38	12.53	12.69	12.84	13.00	13.15	13.31	13.47
	11.54	11.69	11.85	12.00	12.16	12.31	12.47	12.63	12.79	12.95	13.11
	11.21	11.37	11.52	11.68	11.84	12.00	12.16	12.33	12.49	12.65	12.82
	10.93	11.09	11.25	11.41	11.57	11.74	11.90	12.07	12.23	12.40	12.57
	10.69	10.85	11.02	11.18	11.35	11.51	11.68	11.85	12.02	12.19	12.36
	10.49	10.65	10.82	10.98	11.15	11.32	11.49	11.66	11.83	12.00	12.18
	10.31	10.47	10.64	10.81	10.98	11.15	11.33	11.50	11.67	11.85	12.03
20	10.15	10.32	10.49	10.66	10.84	11.01	11.19	11.36	11.54	11.72	11.89
	10.02	10.19	10.36	10.54	10.71	10.89	11.06	11.24	11.42	11.60	11.78
	9.90	10.07	10.25	10.42	10.60	10.78	10.96	11.14	11.32	11.50	11.69
	9.79	9.97	10.15	10.33	10.51	10.69	10.87	11.05	11.23	11.42	11.60
	9.70	9.88	10.06	10.24	10.42	10.60	10.79	10.97	11.16	11.34	11.53
	9.62	9.80	9.98	10.16	10.35	10.53	10.72	10.90	11.09	11.28	11.47
	9.55	9.73	9.91	10.10	10.28	10.47	10.66	10.84	11.03	11.22	11.41
	9.49	9.67	9.85	10.04	10.23	10.41	10.60	10.79	10.98	11.17	11.37
	9.43	9.61	9.80	9.99	10.18	10.37	10.56	10.75	10.94	11.13	11.32
	9.38	9.57	9.75	9.94	10.13	10.32	10.52	10.71	10.90	11.09	11.29
30	9.33	9.52	9.71	9.90	10.09	10.29	10.48	10.67	10.87	11.06	11.26

years

	13.50	13.75	14.00	14.25	14.50	14.75	15.00	15.25	15.50	15.75	16.00 %
1	89.55	89.67	89.79	89.90	90.02	90.14	90.26	90.38	90.49	90.61	90.73
	47.78	47.89	48.01	48.13	48.25	48.37	48.49	48.61	48.72	48.84	48.96
	33.94	34.06	34.18	34.30	34.42	34.54	34.67	34.79	34.91	35.03	35.16
	27.08	27.20	27.33	27.45	27.58	27.70	27.83	27.96	28.08	28.21	28.34
5	23.01	23.14	23.27	23.40	23.53	23.66	23.79	23.92	24.05	24.19	24.32
	20.34	20.47	20.61	20.74	20.87	21.01	21.15	21.28	21.42	21.55	21.69
	18.46	18.60	18.74	18.88	19.02	19.16	19.30	19.44	19.58	19.72	19.86
	17.09	17.23	17.37	17.51	17.66	17.80	17.95	18.09	18.24	18.38	18.53
	16.04	16.19	16.33	16.48	16.63	16.78	16.92	17.07	17.22	17.37	17.53
10	15.23	15.38	15.53	15.68	15.83	15.98	16.13	16.29	16.44	16.60	16.75
	14.58	14.73	14.89	15.04	15.20	15.35	15.51	15.67	15.82	15.98	16.14
	14.06	14.21	14.37	14.53	14.69	14.85	15.01	15.17	15.33	15.49	15.66
	13.63	13.79	13.95	14.11	14.28	14.44	14.60	14.77	14.93	15.10	15.27
	13.28	13.44	13.60	13.77	13.94	14.10	14.27	14.44	14.61	14.78	14.95
	12.98	13.15	13.32	13.49	13.66	13.83	14.00	14.17	14.34	14.51	14.69
	12.74	12.91	13.08	13.25	13.42	13.59	13.77	13.94	14.12	14.29	14.47
	12.53	12.70	12.87	13.05	13.22	13.40	13.58	13.75	13.93	14.11	14.29
	12.35	12.53	12.70	12.88	13.06	13.24	13.42	13.60	13.78	13.96	14.14
	12.20	12.38	12.56	12.74	12.92	13.10	13.28	13.46	13.65	13.83	14.02
20	12.07	12.25	12.44	12.62	12.80	12.98	13.17	13.35	13.54	13.73	13.91
	11.96	12.15	12.33	12.51	12.70	12.88	13.07	13.26	13.45	13.64	13.82
	11.87	12.05	12.24	12.43	12.61	12.80	12.99	13.18	13.37	13.56	13.75
	11.79	11.97	12.16	12.35	12.54	12.73	12.92	13.11	13.30	13.49	13.69
	11.72	11.91	12.10	12.29	12.48	12.67	12.86	13.05	13.25	13.44	13.63
	11.66	11.85	12.04	12.23	12.42	12.61	12.81	13.00	13.20	13.39	13.59
	11.60	11.80	11.99	12.18	12.38	12.57	12.76	12.96	13.16	13.35	13.55
	11.56	11.75	11.95	12.14	12.34	12.53	12.73	12.92	13.12	13.32	13.52
	11.52	11.71	11.91	12.10	12.30	12.50	12.70	12.89	13.09	13.29	13.49
	11.48	11.68	11.88	12.07	12.27	12.47	12.67	12.87	13.07	13.27	13.47
30	11.45	11.65	11.85	12.05	12.25	12.44	12.64	12.84	13.05	13.25	13.45

years

APPENDIX II
FHA Estimated Closing Costs

These are not the actual closing costs a borrower will pay but are figures that are used to calculate FHA maximum loan amounts. See the FHA chapter for details.

Property Value	Closing Costs All Oregon except Washington County	Closing Costs Washington County only
$ 15,000 - 19,999	$550	$550
20,000 - 24,999	600	600
25,000 - 29,999	650	650
30,000 - 34,999	700	700
35,000 - 39,999	750	800
40,000 - 44,999	800	850
45,000 - 49,999	900	900
50,000 - 54,999	950	1000
55,000 - 59,999	1000	1050
60,000 - 64,999	1050	1150
65,000 - 69,999	1150	1150
70,000 - 74,999	1200	1250
75,000 - 79,999	1250	1300
80,000 - 84,999	1300	1350
85,000 - 89,999	1350	1400
90,000 - 94,999	1400	1450
95,000 - 99,999	1450	1500
100,000 -104,999	1500	1550
105,000 -109,999	1550	1600
110,000 -114,999	1600	1700
115,000 -119,999	1700	1750
120,000 -124,999	1750	1800
125,000 -129,999	1800	1850
130,000 -134,999	1850	1900
135,000 -139,999	1900	1950
140,000 -144,999	1950	2000
145,000 -149,999	2000	2050
150,000 -154,999	2050	2150
155,000 -159,999	2100	2200

APPENDIX III
Sample Title Insurance Rates

Policy Value	Owner's Policy	Mortgagee's ALTA Policy
$30,000	$215.00	$78.75
$40,000	$255.00	$88.75
$50,000	$295.00	$98.75
$60,000	$325.00	$106.25
$70,000	$355.00	$113.75
$80,000	$385.00	$121.25
$90,000	$415.00	$128.75
$100,000	$445.00	$136.25
$110,000	$470.00	$142.50
$120,000	$495.00	$148.75
$130,000	$520.00	$155.00
$150,000	$570.00	$167.50
$175,000	$632.50	$183.00
$200,000	$695.00	$198.75
$225,000	$757.50	$214.25
$250,000	$820.00	$230.00
$300,000	$945.00	$261.25

Value of Owner's Policy is the sales price; value of Mortgagee's Policy is the loan amount.

DVA requires a standard mortgagee's policy, not an ALTA policy. Cost for this is $25.00.

Rates provided through the courtesy of Stewart Title.

APPENDIX IV

Homeowner's Insurance: Sample Rates

These are sample rates for homeowner's insurance throughout Oregon. They will vary, however, with different policies and insurance companies. Use this chart (or rates from your own insurance agent) when doing calculations for loan qualification.

1. Determine which zone the property is in. (See list below).
2. Contact local fire department to learn the town class rating.
3. Use the appropriate chart below to estimate the yearly premium for homeowner's insurance. (Includes $100 deductible, replacement cost coverage of contents and dwelling, wood-frame construction.)

ZONES:
Zone 2: City of Portland
Zone 3: Benton, Douglas, Josephine, Lane & Lincoln counties
Zone 4: Multnomah county (excluding Portland)
Zone 5: Remainder of the state

Insured Value	ZONE 2 Town Class 2		ZONE 3 Town Class				
			2-4	5-6	7-8	9	10
$50,000	$171		$138	$153	$194	$325	$381
$75,000	$223		$180	$199	$252	$424	$496
$100,000	$293		$237	$262	$332	$558	$653
$150,000	$442		$356	$393	$499	$838	$982

Insured Value	ZONE 4 Town Class					ZONE 5 Town Class				
	2-4	5-6	7-8	9	10	2-4	5-6	7-8	9	10
$50,000	$171	$189	$240	$403	$472	$148	$163	$208	$350	$409
$75,000	$223	$245	$313	$523	$613	$193	$213	$271	$454	$532
$100,000	$293	$322	$412	$689	$806	$254	$281	$357	$598	$700
$150,000	$442	$484	$619	1036	1213	$383	$422	$536	$899	1053

Rates provided through the courtesy of Margie Jones, Allstate Insurance, Washington Square, Portland.

INDEX

BOOK ORDER FORM

Panoply Press, Inc.
P. O. Box 1885
Lake Oswego, Oregon 97034

Please send the following:

_____ copies of How To FINANCE A HOME In Oregon ($12.95)

Add $1.00 per order for postage and handling. Payment must accompany order.

Enclosed is a check or money order in the amount of $ _____

Name _____

Address _____

City _____ State _____ Zip _____

- -

BOOK ORDER FORM

Panoply Press, Inc.
P. O. Box 1885
Lake Oswego, Oregon 97034

Please send the following:

_____ copies of How To FINANCE A HOME In Oregon ($12.95)

Add $1.00 per order for postage and handling. Payment must accompany order.

Enclosed is a check or money order in the amount of $ _____

Name _____

Address _____

City _____ State _____ Zip _____